MUSIATA AKAFEKWA

The Power of Platonic Love

A Handbook for Modern Relationships

Contents

Chapter 1: The Nature of Love

Love is a mystery that has haunted and enchanted humanity for ages. It's a force that ignites passion, inspires art, and drives us to the edge of our sanity. But even with its prevalence, love remains a perplexing enigma, a puzzle we yearn to solve.

In these pages, I invite you to embark on a journey into the labyrinth of love, guided by the wisdom of one of the greatest minds in history: Plato. Through his profound philosophy of love, Plato unravels the mysteries of this primal emotion, shedding light on its nature, its significance in our lives, and how we can pursue it with purpose.

We will explore the many facets of love, from the ethereal realm of Platonic love to the tempestuous passion that sets our hearts ablaze. We will delve into the depths of desire, unraveling the psychology behind our yearning for connection, and illuminating the crucial role of friendship in our pursuit of love's meaning.

Drawing inspiration from the ancient traditions of Greece, we will uncover the art of courtship - the delicate dance of flirtation, the intricacies of attraction, and the rituals of wooing. We will examine the profound connection between love and beauty, exploring how they intertwine in our hearts and minds.

But this is not merely an intellectual pursuit. Throughout these pages, I urge you to reflect on your own experiences of love - its joys, its sorrows, its complexities. I challenge you to question your assumptions, to ponder the lessons that Plato's philosophy can offer, and to embark on your own voyage of self-discovery and understanding.

So let us journey forth into the realm of love, guided by the timeless wisdom of Plato. In our pursuit of this universal human experience, we may uncover profound insights that will forever change how we perceive and embrace love in our lives.

Love, that elusive and enigmatic force, has been portrayed in movies and TV shows as a beautiful and magical phenomenon, capable of conquering all obstacles and bestowing eternal happiness upon us. But the truth is, love is far more complex and multifaceted than such idealistic depictions would have us believe.

In this modern age, where dating apps and online dating have become the norm, we put ourselves out there for the world to judge and potentially reject us, making love a source of fear and apprehension. The high rates of divorce and heartbreak serve as a harsh reminder that love can sometimes be downright terrifying, leaving us feeling shattered and alone, as if we are navigating treacherous waters with no compass.

But love is not all doom and gloom. It can also be a source of joy, comfort, and companionship, providing us with a sense of purpose and fulfillment that is difficult to find elsewhere. Even in the darkest moments, when it feels like all hope is lost, love has the power to lift us up and breathe new life into our souls.

Imagine a modern-day Plato, sitting in a bustling coffee shop, his long beard stroked thoughtfully as he contemplates the mysteries of the universe. In this world of smartphones, social media, and dating apps, his ancient wisdom still rings true: love is the key to everything.

Plato believed that love was not just a fleeting feeling or emotion, but a force that could guide us towards the divine. Love was the very essence of life itself, the glue that held the universe together. However, in our modern times, with the complexities of dating and the constant bombardment of romantic comedies and love songs, one may question Plato's understanding of love. After all, what did he really know about the challenges of modern relationships?

Despite the changes in our world, Plato's ideas about love still resonate today. We continue to believe in the transformative power of love, the way it can uplift us to the heavens and beyond, and how it can unlock the mysteries of the universe.

Love is like a river that flows through our lives, sometimes calm and serene, and at other times turbulent and perilous. We are like boats, navigating the treacherous waters of love, constantly seeking the safest route to our destination, even when we know the risks that lie ahead.

And yet, despite the uncertainties and vulnerabilities that love entails, we keep coming back to it. Like a river that carves its way through the landscape, love has the power to shape and mold us into something new and beautiful. It can bring us boundless joy and happiness, but it can also leave us heartbroken and adrift.

Perhaps it's the thrill of the unknown, the excitement of the journey, that draws us to love. Or maybe it's something deeper, ingrained in our DNA, compelling us to seek out a connection with others, to feel a sense of belonging and purpose in this vast and often lonely world.

Whatever the reason, we continue to pursue love with an unwavering fervor that borders on madness. We watch romantic comedies, swipe through dating apps, and dissect every text message and emoji. We may not always fully comprehend why we are so captivated by love, but we know that it is an intrinsic part of the human experience.

So what is it that makes love so irresistible? Is it the promise of a lifelong companion who will stand by our side through thick and thin? Is it the thrill of discovering new facets of ourselves through our relationships? Or is it simply the joy of sharing our lives with someone who understands us in a way that no one else can?

Perhaps the answer lies in a combination of all these factors, along with countless others that are unique to each individual's experience.

Chapter 2: Beyond Romance - The Complexities of Platonic Love

Love is a powerful force that shapes our lives in ways both expected and unexpected. In this chapter, we'll explore the nuances and complexities of platonic love - the love that exists beyond the romantic sphere. We'll examine the ancient Greek concept of platonic love, which emphasizes emotional and intellectual connections over physical attraction.

Throughout our lives, we form countless relationships with the people around us - some of them romantic, and others strictly platonic. But what exactly does it mean to have a platonic relationship? Is it simply a lack of physical attraction, or is there something more to it?

We will look at the intricacies of platonic love - exploring what it means, how it differs from other forms of love, and the ways in which it can manifest in our lives. We won't just be examining dry theories and definitions - instead, we'll be looking at real-life examples that illustrate the complexities of platonic love.

From the bonds of lifelong friendships to the moments of connection we share with strangers, we'll explore the different ways in which platonic love can take shape. We'll discuss the unique challenges and rewards that come with these types of relationships, and consider how they can help us to grow and evolve as individuals.

So, if you're ready to take a deep dive into the world of platonic love, buckle up and get ready for a journey through the complexities of this powerful and transformative force.

I Defining Platonic Love

Plato explored the nature of love extensively in his dialogues, particularly in his Symposium[1] and Phaedrus. In the Symposium, Plato presents a group of characters who gather to discuss the nature of love, with Socrates leading the discussion. In the dialogue, Socrates describes how he learned about love from the prophetess Diotima, who taught him that love is not just a desire for beauty, but a desire for the eternal and the divine.

Plato's ideas about love were not limited to just romantic love, but also included the love between friends, family members, and even strangers. He believed that all forms of love were interconnected and could ultimately lead to a greater understanding of the world and ourselves.

One of Plato's famous quotes about love comes from the Symposium: "Love is born into every human being; it calls back the halves of our original nature together; it tries to make one out of two and heal the wound of human nature." This

---

[1] (Plato. 2008. *Symposium*. Translated by Robin Waterfield. N.p.: OUP Oxford.)

quote emphasizes the idea that love has the power to bring people together and help them become whole.

In modern times, the concept of platonic love has evolved to include a broader range of non-romantic relationships, such as close friendships, mentor-mentee relationships, and even admiration for public figures or celebrities. While physical attraction may still play a role in some of these relationships, the emphasis is on emotional and intellectual connections, similar to the ancient Greek concept of platonic love.

In contrast to modern definitions of love, which often place a heavy emphasis on physical attraction and sexual desire, platonic love prioritizes emotional and intellectual connections between two individuals. It is a deep and meaningful bond that is built on shared experiences, interests, and values, rather than just physical attraction.

For example, think of a long-term friendship that has lasted for years, where two individuals have built a strong connection through shared experiences and mutual interests. Despite not having any romantic or sexual attraction towards each other, they still share a deep and meaningful bond that is often stronger than some romantic relationships. For example, in modern times, we might hear the phrase "Bro's before ho's" A contemporary example of platonic love.

Another example of platonic love can be seen in the bond between a parent and child. The love between a parent and child is often based on the emotional and intellectual connections between them, rather than just physical attraction. The bond between them is built on shared experiences, values, and a deep sense of trust and respect.

Overall, platonic love is a type of love that goes beyond physical attraction and is based on emotional and intellectual connections. It is a deep and meaningful bond that can exist between friends, family members, and even strangers, and is often seen as a purer form of love than romantic love.

II. Examples of Platonic Love

In this section, we will explore the different forms of platonic love and their unique rewards and limitations.

A. Platonic Love Between Friends

Plato believed that true friendship was the highest form of platonic love, as it was based on shared values and a deep intellectual connection,[2]. In his Symposium, Plato depicts Socrates discussing the nature of love with his friends, including the philosopher Aristophanes, who tells the story of how humans were once double creatures with four arms and four legs, until Zeus split them in two, creating the modern human and condemning them to a lifetime of searching for their other half. According to Aristophanes, the longing for our other half is what drives us to seek out love and connection.

In contemporary society, we can see examples of platonic love between friends in many different contexts. For instance, a group of college roommates who have lived together and shared experiences for several years may develop a deep bond based on their mutual understanding and support. Similarly, coworkers who collaborate on projects and share a sense of camaraderie may form a platonic love bond that lasts beyond

---

[2] (Plato. 2008. *Symposium*. Translated by Robin Waterfield. N.p.: OUP Oxford.)

their time at the company.

However, some scholars argue that platonic love between friends can be limiting, as it can reinforce existing power structures and exclude those who do not fit into established social groups[3]. For instance, Bell Hooks has argued that traditional notions of friendship can be exclusionary, as they are often based on shared experiences of privilege and may exclude marginalized individuals. Despite these limitations, platonic love between friends remains an important aspect of human connection, offering support, understanding, and a sense of belonging.

B. Platonic Love Between Family Members

Plato's notion that emotional and intellectual connections are more important than physical attraction applies not only to romantic love but also to the love between family members. As per Plato, love is a universal force that binds all individuals together, connecting them to something greater than themselves. Platonic love between family members is not just a matter of biology but a profound emotional and intellectual connection that evolves over time.

Contemporary examples of this type of love can be seen in the strong bonds between siblings who support and care for one another throughout their lives. Take the Williams sisters, Serena and Venus, for instance - their relationship epitomizes platonic love between family members. They have been each

---

[3] (Hooks, Bell. 1994. *Seduction and Betrayal: Women and Literature.* N.p.: New York: William Morrow and Company, Inc.)

other's most fervent supporters through thick and thin, despite their competitive natures.

While some modern scholars argue that physical attraction is necessary for love to exist, including familial love, Plato's emphasis on platonic love remains strong. There are those who argue that platonic love between family members can be just as powerful, if not more so, than romantic or sexual love.

Despite the differing views on the nature of platonic love between family members, it remains a crucial and intricate type of love that influences our lives and relationships. It is a bond that provides support and solace in times of need, yet it also has its limitations and challenges.

C. Platonic Love Between Strangers

Platonic love can also be found in the connections we make with strangers. From the kind stranger who offers a helping hand during a difficult time to the unexpected connection made with someone on a plane, platonic love between strangers can be fleeting but powerful. As Plato said, "Love is born into every human being; it calls back the halves of our original nature together; it tries to make one out of two and heal the wound of human nature".

Platonic love between strangers can manifest in various ways, such as through acts of kindness and empathy towards others. For instance, a recent study by Oliver Scott Curry and colleagues found that people tend to show kindness and cooperation towards strangers, as a way of promoting social connections and building trust[4]. In a world where strangers are often viewed with suspicion and mistrust, platonic love can help to bridge the divide and promote greater social harmony.

However, the limitations of platonic love between strangers should not be overlooked. Misunderstandings and miscommunications can easily arise when there is no shared history or mutual understanding between individuals. Additionally, some scholars have argued that the emphasis on platonic love between strangers can be problematic, as it can detract from the importance of cultivating deeper, long-lasting relationships[5].

To illustrate the power of platonic love between strangers, consider the allegory of the Good Samaritan. In this parable, a man is beaten and left for dead on the side of the road. Two men who pass by him, a priest and a Levite, ignore him and continue on their way. However, a Samaritan, a stranger to the man and of a different social and religious background, stops to help him, providing him with aid and comfort (Luke 10:25-37). The story highlights the power of human connection and the capacity for strangers to show compassion and empathy towards one another.

In contrast, some modern scholars argue for alternative relationship types that contradict and challenge the traditional notion of platonic love. For example, Elizabeth Brake argues for the value of "minimal marriage," which emphasizes the importance of intimate relationships that do not necessarily conform to traditional marriage norms. Such alternative

---

[4] Curry, O. S., M. J. Chesters, and C. J. Van Lissa. 2019. "Cooperation in context: Public goods games and post-socialist societies." *Journal of Cross-Cultural Psychology* 50 (2): 242-266.

[5] Nussbaum, Martha C. 2018. *The Therapy of Desire: Theory and Practice in Hellenistic Ethics*. N.p.: Princeton University Press.

relationship types suggest that the traditional emphasis on platonic love may not be the only or most desirable form of human connection.

Through examining the unique rewards and limitations of each type of platonic love, we can gain a greater understanding of the complexities and nuances of human relationships, and appreciate the power and potential[6] of platonic love to enrich our lives.

III. The Challenges of Platonic Love

Platonic love, much like any other relationship, is not without its complexities. It demands a significant amount of effort, patience, and understanding to keep it afloat. When navigating the uncharted waters of platonic love, it is common to encounter challenges such as jealousy, misunderstandings, and unrequited love. As Plato himself once said, "At the touch of love, everyone becomes a poet." However, not every love story has a happy ending, and the challenges of platonic love can leave one feeling like a poet with no muse. To illustrate this point, the allegory of the Cave from Plato's Republic[7] comes to mind. Just as the prisoners in the cave struggled to adjust to the bright light of the outside world, we too can struggle to adapt to the complexities of platonic love.

Jealousy is a complex emotion that can be difficult to manage in any type of relationship, including platonic ones. It can arise

---

[6] Brake, Elizabeth. 2012. "Minimizing Marriage: Marriage, Morality, and the Law,Studies in Feminist Philosophy." *Oxford Academic*, (May). 10.1093.

[7] Anderson, Albert A., trans. 2001. *Plato's Republic, Books 1-10*. N.p.: Agora Publications, Incorporated.

when one person perceives that the other is becoming closer to someone else or is devoting less time to the friendship. This can lead to feelings of betrayal and insecurity, which can strain the relationship. In the allegory of the charioteer in Plato's Phaedrus, Socrates describes the soul as having two horses, one noble and one ignoble, which represent the rational and irrational parts of the human psyche.

The charioteer must guide both horses to the divine realm of knowledge, but the ignoble horse can become unruly and difficult to control, leading to a bumpy ride. Similarly, in platonic love, jealousy can be like the ignoble horse, causing turbulence in the friendship.

However, as Alcibiades describes in Plato's Symposium, despite his jealous feelings towards Socrates, he maintained a deep friendship with him, which speaks to the resilience and strength of platonic love.

Misunderstandings can also pose a challenge in platonic relationships. Different communication styles or misunderstandings about expectations can lead to hurt feelings or resentment. For example, one person in a friendship may believe that they are giving more than they are receiving, leading to feelings of imbalance and dissatisfaction.

Platonic relationships are not immune to the complexities of unrequited love, which can present a significant challenge. The experience of developing romantic feelings for a friend who does not reciprocate can be excruciatingly painful.

Plato's "Symposium" tells the story of Aristophanes, who speaks of how humans were once double creatures. This allegory illustrates the longing and yearning for completion that drives us towards love. However, when unrequited love arises in a platonic relationship, it can cause confusion, pain, and an unbalanced power dynamic. It can be challenging to navigate these feelings while maintaining the friendship, and sometimes, it may be necessary to take a step back to heal and reassess the relationship.

Despite these challenges, platonic love can also evolve and change over time. Friendships can deepen as both people grow and change, developing new interests and shared experiences. Platonic love can also shift in response to life changes, such as moving to a new city or experiencing a major life event. For example, a friend may become a source of support during a difficult time, strengthening the bond between them.

Platonic love is not without its challenges, and it takes a brave soul to navigate the murky waters of friendship. Personal stories can bring these challenges to life, like the tale of a person who has harbored romantic feelings for their best friend for years, only to finally confess their love and risk everything they had built. Or the story of two friends who struggle to communicate, leading to misunderstandings and hurt feelings that threaten to tear them apart. These are the moments that test the strength and resilience of platonic love, and the ones that make it all the more rewarding in the end.

The truth is, platonic love is not for the faint of heart. It's not all rainbows and butterflies, and it's certainly not a simple walk in the park. But that's the beauty of it. The challenges, the misunderstandings, the unrequited feelings, and the jealousies - they all add up to something far greater than a surface-level connection. It's about embracing the messiness of life and finding comfort in the imperfections of our relationships. Through it all, platonic love can lead to a deep sense of fulfillment and an unbreakable bond with those who matter most. It's not always easy, but it's always worth it.

IV. The Rewards of Platonic Love

Platonic love can be a refreshing oasis in the desert of life, quenching our thirst for human connection. Just as a hummingbird sips nectar from a flower, we can draw sustenance from our platonic relationships, finding comfort and support during the harsh winds of life's challenges. These relationships can act as a mirror, reflecting the best parts of ourselves back to us, like a lighthouse that guides ships through a treacherous sea. By nurturing our platonic relationships, we can grow and evolve, like a caterpillar that transforms into a butterfly, ready to spread its wings and soar. And just as a treasure hunter finds a precious gem, personal anecdotes can illustrate the richness and beauty of these rewarding relationships.

Platonic love is a garden of endless possibilities, where each flower blooms with its own unique beauty. Personal anecdotes reveal the depth and diversity of the rewards that come with platonic relationships. It might be a friend who acts as a beacon of light, illuminating the path ahead when we find ourselves lost in the dark. It could also be a mentor who serves as a sculptor, chiseling away the rough edges and helping us to become the best versions of ourselves. And sometimes, the sweetest reward can come from a stranger who, like a gentle rain, provides comfort and relief in the midst of life's droughts.

Platonic love is like a seed that, when nurtured, can grow into a beautiful and resilient plant. It has the power to push us out of our comfort zones, like a gust of wind that carries us to new heights. As we navigate the twists and turns of life, platonic love can be a beacon of light that illuminates our path, guiding us towards growth, evolution, and self-discovery. It can teach us to see the world through a different lens, broadening our horizons and expanding our perspectives. Through the challenges and triumphs of platonic love, we can become better, stronger, and more compassionate individuals.

Platonic love is like a hidden gem, waiting to be unearthed and treasured. It can bring us a wealth of emotional riches, like a rainbow of precious gems glistening in the sun. As Plato once said, "Love is born into every human being; it calls back the halves of our original nature together; it tries to make one out of two and heal the wound of human nature." Platonic love shows us that we don't need a knight in shining armor or a fairy tale romance to feel fulfilled. The genuine love and support of a true friend can be just as rewarding and valuable, like a rare diamond found in a sea of pebbles.

V. Continuing the Journey of Love

As we near the final pages of this chapter, let us not forget that platonic love is the beating pulse of our human existence, a vital force that propels us forward. The rewards and challenges of platonic love are like the ebbs and flows of a tumultuous ocean, sometimes calm and sometimes tumultuous. But it is the tempest that reveals the hidden treasures of the deep, the secrets of the heart, the power of trust and vulnerability that can only be unearthed through the challenges of platonic love. We must cherish and nurture these connections if we are to truly experience the beauty and complexity of life.

As we navigate the complexities of modern life, the idea of platonic love may seem elusive, like a butterfly that we can see but can never quite catch. However, research has shown that building and maintaining strong platonic relationships is essential to our well-being and happiness. As Dr. Emma

Seppala, a well-known psychologist, notes, "Social connection is such a basic feature of human experience that when we are deprived of it, we suffer physically, mentally, and emotionally."[8]

Indeed, in today's world of superficial online connections and fleeting social media likes, true platonic love can seem like a rare and precious gem. But it is worth the effort to seek out and nurture those genuine connections that provide us with comfort, support, and inspiration. For as Seppala goes on to explain, "Cultivating social connection is not just good for us, it's a basic human need."

As we conclude this chapter, we are reminded that love is an ever-evolving journey, like a river that constantly changes course and shape. Just as we must adapt to the twists and turns of a winding river, we must also navigate the complexities of love with an open heart and a willingness to learn. So let us forge ahead into the next chapter, like intrepid explorers, eager to uncover new insights and revelations about the mysteries of the heart. For the journey of love is one that never truly ends, and we are all just passengers on this wild and wonderful ride.

---

[8] Seppala, Emma. 2017. "The science of connection: The health benefits of social connection." Berkeley Wellness, University of California. https://ww w.berkeleywellness.com/healthy-mind/mind-body/article/science-connec tion.

Chapter 3: The Psychology of Desire —How Love Shapes Our Lives

As Plato once said, "At the touch of love, everyone becomes a poet." Indeed, love has the power to shape our desires and influence our behavior in profound ways. In this chapter, we will explore the psychology of desire and how it relates to love. We will examine the concepts of desire and attraction, and how they can both drive us towards love and complicate our relationships. Join me as I delve into the mysteries of the heart and uncover the ways in which love shapes our lives.

I: How love shapes our desires and influences our behavior

Love has the power to shape our desires and influence our behavior in profound ways, leading us down paths we never thought possible. From the rush of dopamine that floods our brains when we first fall in love to the deeper, more complex emotions that develop over time, love has the ability to transform us from the inside out.

Indeed, recent research in psychology has shed light on just how powerful the influence of love can be. For example, a study published in the journal Social Cognitive and Affective Neuroscience found that the same brain regions involved in addiction were also activated when people viewed pictures of their romantic partners. Similarly, a study published in the journal Emotion found that people who were deeply in love showed increased activity in brain regions associated with reward and motivation when they viewed pictures of their partners.

But love is not just about the rush of attraction and desire. It can also shape our desires and influence our behavior in more subtle ways. For example, when we are in a committed relationship, our desire for experiences and opportunities outside of that relationship may decrease, as we prioritize our partner and the bond we have built with them. Love can also influence the way we perceive ourselves and our place in the world, shaping our goals and ambitions in ways we may not even realize.

In the next section, we will delve deeper into the concepts of desire and attraction, exploring how these powerful forces shape our experiences of love and influence the paths we take in life.

II. Overview of the concepts of desire and attraction

Desire is a hungry beast, always prowling and searching for its next meal. It compels us to pursue our deepest passions and yearnings, driving us ever forward towards our goals. Attraction, on the other hand, is like a siren song that we cannot resist, beckoning us towards certain people or experiences.

Even the great philosopher Plato understood the irresistible allure of desire and attraction, using his allegory of the cave to illustrate how we are drawn towards the light of truth and beauty. Today, we can see the power of these concepts in our own lives, from the burning desire to succeed in our careers to the magnetic attraction we feel towards someone we love.

Desire and attraction are like two sides of the same coin, both interwoven and inseparable. They are not solely based on physical appearances, as emotional and intellectual connections are just as significant in shaping our desires and attractions towards others. For instance, a person may be drawn to someone because of their ability to understand and empathize with their feelings, or their shared love for a particular hobby. Recent scientific research supports this, as studies have found that individuals with similar values and beliefs are more likely to develop long-lasting relationships[9]. In the end, it's not just about looks, but about the deeper connections we form with others that truly shape our desires and attractions.

According to a recent study by Acevedo and Aron, emotional and intellectual connections are just as important as physical attraction in the formation of desire and attraction. The researchers found that "individuals who reported high levels of perceived emotional similarity with their partners had greater relationship satisfaction and commitment," highlighting the importance of emotional connections in romantic relationships[10]. Additionally, individuals who reported sharing more

---

[9] Meyer, and Lieberman. 2011. The Oxford Handbook of Social Neuroscience. Edited by Jean Decety and John T. Cacioppo. N.p.: Oxford University Press.

[10] Acevedo, B. P., and A. Aron. 2009. "Does a long-term relationship kill romantic love?" *Review of General Psychology* 13 (1): 59-65.

activities and interests with their partners were more likely to report higher levels of desire and attraction. This suggests that desire and attraction are complex and multifaceted concepts that involve both physical and emotional components.

The complexity of desire and attraction is also evident in the way they can change over time. What we desire and are attracted to in our youth may differ from what we desire and are attracted to in our later years. This can be influenced by factors such as life experiences, societal norms, and personal growth.

Despite their complexity, desire and attraction are integral to our understanding of love and how it shapes our lives. As we continue to explore the psychology of desire, we will delve deeper into the science behind these concepts and how they affect our behavior in relationships.

III. The Dark Side of Desire

Picture this: a man, let's call him James, who is madly in love with a woman he cannot have. She is his friend, his confidant, but nothing more, for she is already committed to another. James is consumed by an unquenchable desire for her, and the more he tries to suppress it, the stronger it grows.

Slowly but surely, James' obsession with this woman begins to take over his life. He is unable to think of anything else but her, and he begins to lose sight of reality. He imagines scenarios where she leaves her partner and runs away with him, or where he confesses his love and she reciprocates. In his mind, their love is destined to be, but in reality, it is nothing but a destructive fantasy.

As James' desire for this woman grows stronger, so does

his jealousy of her partner. He becomes obsessed with every little detail of their relationship, picking apart their flaws and highlighting his own supposed superiority. He isolates himself from other friends, convinced that he needs to be near her at all times, even if it's just as a friend.

In the end, James' unfulfilled desires for this woman lead him down a path of darkness and despair. His obsession with her consumes him, leaving nothing but a hollow shell of a man behind. The allure of unfulfilled desires can be powerful, but it can also be dangerous, as James' tragic story illustrates. As Plato warned us long ago, desire can be the cause of all evil, and in matters of the heart, the consequences of unfulfilled desires can be devastating.

Jealousy is a common negative effect of unfulfilled desires, which can quickly turn into an all-consuming obsession, leading to destructive behavior and even violence. As Plato once said, "At the touch of love, everyone becomes a poet," but it's important to note that love, or rather, unrequited love, can also lead to destructive behavior. A study conducted by Joel Wade and colleagues (2009)[11] found that individuals who experienced unrequited love were more likely to engage in stalking and other intrusive behaviors. These behaviors often stem from the intense emotions that come with unfulfilled desires, including jealousy, obsession, and the need for control.

Platonic love, too, can have negative effects when unfulfilled. Platonic love refers to the love between friends, without any romantic or sexual attraction. However, when one friend

---

[11] Wade, T. J., L. K. Butrie, K. M. Hoffman, and R. L. Michalski. n.d. "Unrequited love: On heartbreak, anger, guilt, scriptlessness, and humiliation." *Journal of Social and Personal Relationships*, no. 26, 377-400. 10.1177.

desires more from the relationship than the other, jealousy and resentment can develop. In extreme cases, the friendship can end altogether.

It's clear that unfulfilled desires, whether in love or other areas of life, can have negative consequences. As we delve deeper into the dark side of desire, we must keep in mind the potential dangers of allowing our wants and needs to consume us.

Obsession can be a perilous path, leading individuals to lose sight of reality and become consumed by their desires. When someone becomes fixated on something or someone, they can quickly spiral into madness. Obsessive behavior is often driven by intense emotions that come with unfulfilled desires, such as jealousy, possessiveness, and the need for control. According to a study conducted by Turchik and Garske (2009)[12]Individuals who experience obsessive love are more likely to engage in stalking and other intrusive behaviors. But obsession is not only limited to romantic relationships. It can also manifest in other areas of life, such as work or hobbies. The novel "The Shining" highlights the destructive power of obsession with the repeated phrase "All work and no play makes Jack a dull boy." This phrase illustrates the dark and dangerous cycle of obsession and how it can take over a person's life, leading them to commit heinous acts.

Addiction is yet another negative consequence of unfulfilled desires. The allure of something that cannot be obtained can be overpowering, leading to a relentless pursuit that consumes

---

[12] Turchik, J. A., and J. P. Garske. n.d. "Probing the Depths of Intrapersonal Stalking: The Role of Attachment and Emotional Regulation in Predicting Stalking Propensity." *Journal of Interpersonal Violence* 24 (10): 1594-1613. 10.1177.

the individual. In contemporary times, the rise of social media has made it easier to indulge in addictive behavior, such as compulsive scrolling or online shopping. However, the consequences of addiction can be severe, affecting both physical and mental health. Plato's concept of platonic love serves as an allegory for the dangers of addiction - just as one can become addicted to the idea of a platonic love that cannot be fulfilled, so too can one become addicted to something else that remains out of reach.

In summary, unfulfilled desires can have a dark and dangerous side. The negative effects of jealousy, obsession, and addiction can be all-consuming, leaving individuals as empty shells. As Plato once warned, desire can be the root of all evil. It is up to each individual to control their desires and not let them control us, lest we fall prey to their dangerous allure.

IV. The Power of Attraction

Attraction is a force as old as humanity itself, an electric charge that pulls us towards certain people, places, or things. In the context of Platonic love, attraction is the spark that ignites the fire of a deep and meaningful relationship. Plato believed that attraction was not just about physical beauty, but also about the beauty of the soul. He argued that we are drawn to people who embody the virtues we admire and aspire to cultivate within ourselves.

In modern psychology, attraction is seen as a fundamental human experience that drives our social behavior and shapes our relationships. Recent studies have shown that we are more likely to be attracted to people who share our values and beliefs, as well as those who possess qualities that we find desirable, such as confidence, intelligence, or kindness.

Moreover, attraction is not just about the qualities of the other person but also about how we perceive ourselves. The way we see ourselves influences our perception of others and can impact our level of attraction to them. For example, individuals with high self-esteem tend to be more attracted to people who exhibit confidence, while those with lower self-esteem may be drawn to those who show them affection and validation.

Attraction is a complex phenomenon that involves both psychological and physiological factors. Research has shown that attraction triggers the release of dopamine, a neurotransmitter associated with pleasure and reward, in the brain. This chemical response can create a feeling of euphoria and increase our desire to pursue the object of our attraction.

Attraction is like a magnetic force that pulls us towards someone we find appealing. It's an unrelenting urge to be close to them, to touch them, to breathe in their scent. I remember once I met a woman at a coffee shop, and as soon as I laid eyes on her, my heart skipped a beat. We talked for hours, and I couldn't resist the attraction I felt towards her.

That pull was so strong that I found myself doing everything in my power to make her laugh, to impress her, to make her see me as someone worth spending time with. It's incredible how attraction can drive us to be our best selves, to put forth the effort to build a relationship with someone we're drawn to. But it's not just romantic relationships that attraction can impact. It can influence how we interact with our friends, coworkers, and even strangers on the street. When we're attracted to someone, we're more likely to lend a helping hand or offer support, simply because we feel a connection with them. It's a powerful force that shapes our lives in countless ways.

As we explore Plato's philosophy of love, we discover that attraction is not merely a physical phenomenon, but a spiritual one as well. It's about seeking out the beauty and goodness that lies within others, and the quest for self-improvement. This concept is exemplified in the story of John, a struggling artist who had always been drawn to women who possessed a talent for painting.

He found himself enamored with a young painter named Sarah, whose work he admired greatly. As they got to know each other, John realized that Sarah's artistic talent was a reflection of her kind, empathetic nature, and he was drawn to her all the more for it. In this way, Plato's idea of attraction as a means of seeking out qualities that we ourselves aspire to still holds true today, as we continue to seek out partners who possess qualities that we ourselves wish to cultivate.

As much as attraction can bring us closer to the people we admire, it can also lead us down a path of destruction. Take the case of Mark, a young man who was captivated by his girlfriend, Jane. Jane was beautiful and confident, and Mark was infatuated with her from the moment they met. However, as time passed, Mark began to realize that Jane was not the person he thought she was. She was manipulative and abusive, constantly belittling him and controlling his every move. Despite the pain she caused him, Mark couldn't help but stay with Jane, convinced that his love for her was worth the suffering. It wasn't until one fateful night when Jane's anger boiled over, and she lashed out at Mark in a fit of rage, ultimately leading to his tragic demise.

This heartbreaking story serves as a grim reminder of the dangers of uncontrolled attraction. We must always be mindful of the people we allow into our lives and seek help when we find ourselves in dangerous situations.

Attraction is the spark that ignites the fire of our relationships. It's the force that propels us towards those who we believe can complete us, who can bring color to our otherwise monochrome lives. Attraction can show us sides of ourselves we never knew existed, reveal hidden passions we never thought possible. It's the key that unlocks the door to our souls, allowing us to explore our deepest desires with a trusted partner by our side. And in the end, attraction can lead us to a love that lasts a lifetime, painting our world with every shade of the rainbow.

As the dust settles on this topic, it becomes clear that attraction is a force to be reckoned with. It can offer boundless happiness and contentment, yet its darker side can inflict unspeakable suffering on those who fall prey to its clutches. Armed with the knowledge of its impact on our lives and relationships, we can hope to withstand its fierce winds and steer our course towards safer waters.

V. The Evolution of Desire

Imagine, for a moment, a young woman walking through a crowded bar. She notices a man across the room who catches her eye. He stands tall with broad shoulders, a chiseled jawline, and sharp brown eyes. Without even realizing it, her heart rate quickens, her palms start to sweat, and a wave of desire washes over her. It's not just his good looks that she finds attractive; it's also his air of confidence and dominance.

This phenomenon can be explained by the evolutionary origins of desire. According to recent studies, men with more masculine features, such as strong jawlines and deep voices, are perceived as more attractive because they signal good genes and physical health[13]. Similarly, women with hourglass figures and clear skin are seen as more desirable because they indicate fertility and youthfulness[14] .

Attraction is not just limited to physical characteristics; it also encompasses social status and power. For example, in many cultures, men who are wealthy or hold positions of power are seen as highly desirable mates[15]. This desire for status and power can also be seen in modern-day workplaces, where individuals compete for promotions and recognition. Our attraction to those who hold high social status or power is rooted in our desire to pass on advantageous traits to future generations, such as wealth, resources, and social influence.

But how have these instincts shaped human behavior throughout history? One need only look at the countless stories of powerful rulers and wealthy elites taking multiple partners or engaging in extramarital affairs to see how attraction and desire have influenced human behavior. From ancient emperors to modern-day celebrities, the desire for power and status often translates into a desire for sexual conquests. However, as we will see in the next section, this type of behavior is not always beneficial for the individuals involved or for society as a whole.

As human beings, we are all subject to the whims of evolution, and attraction is no exception. Our brains have been wired

---

[13] Fisher, H. n.d. "Lust, attraction, and attachment in mammalian reproduction." *Human Nature,* 9 (1): 23-52. 10.1007/s12110-998-1002-3.

[14] Singh, D., and D. Singh. n.d. "Shape and color matter: A sex-differentiated approach to understanding human beauty." *Evolutionary Psychology* 9 (3): 530-552.

[15]

over millennia to prefer certain traits that signal reproductive fitness and genetic health. Men are instinctively drawn to women who exude signs of youthfulness and fertility, such as a clear complexion, symmetrical facial features, and a waist-to-hip ratio of around 0.7. Women, on the other hand, are naturally attracted to men who display traits that indicate physical prowess and genetic fitness, such as a broad chest, a V-shaped torso, and a deep, resonant voice.

But how do these preferences translate into our modern world? While some evolutionary traits may seem outdated, their influence can still be seen in our behavior and culture. For instance, men are still often drawn to positions of power and prestige, while women are often expected to prioritize child-rearing and domestic responsibilities. While gender roles have evolved over time, their origins can be traced back to our evolutionary past. As we navigate the complexities of modern society, it's important to recognize the ways in which our evolutionary history continues to shape our behavior and preferences[16].

However, not all of our preferences can be explained by evolutionary biology alone. Cultural and social factors also play a role in shaping our attractions and desires. For example, many people are attracted to partners who share their interests and values, or who possess certain personality traits like kindness or a sense of humor. In some cases, our preferences may be influenced by our family or community, or by our exposure to different cultures and media.

---

[16] Buss, D. M. n.d. "Sex differences in human mate preferences: Evolutionary hypotheses tested in 37 cultures." *Behavioral and brain sciences* 12 (01): 1-49. 10.1017/s0140525x00023992.

As we explore the many factors that contribute to our attractions and desires, it's important to keep an open mind and recognize the complex interplay of biology, culture, and individual experience. By understanding the many factors that shape our romantic and sexual preferences, we can better navigate the sometimes confusing and unpredictable landscape of modern dating and relationships.

While modern society has granted us the freedom to choose partners based on more than just physical characteristics, the evolutionary roots of attraction still run deep. Recent studies have shown that emotional and intellectual compatibility play a significant role in partner selection.[17] However, underlying desires for traits that signal genetic fitness and reproductive potential still persist, even if they are often unconscious.

But what about platonic love, which focuses on emotional and intellectual connection rather than physical attraction? It's important to remember that platonic love, while not rooted in sexual desire, is still a form of love that can be deeply fulfilling and meaningful. In fact, some argue that platonic love may even be more profound than romantic love, as it is not based on fleeting physical attraction but on a deep emotional bond.

Regardless of the type of love we seek, understanding the evolutionary origins of desire and attraction can help us navigate the complex landscape of romantic and sexual relationships. By recognizing the powerful forces at play in our minds and bodies, we can make more informed choices and build deeper, more meaningful connections with others.

---

[17] Gonzaga, G. C., B. Campos, and T. Bradbury. n.d. "Similarity, convergence, and relationship satisfaction in dating and married couples." *Journal of personality and social psychology* 93 (1): 34-48. https://doi.org/10.1037/002 2-3514.93.1.34.

Chapter 4: Love and Relationships: Platonic vs. Romantic Love

I magine having a friend who understands every aspect of your personality, from your quirks to your sense of humor. Someone who connects with you on an emotional and intellectual level, providing you with companionship and support that is fulfilling and meaningful. This is the essence of platonic love, a type of love that has been celebrated throughout history. From Plato's "Symposium" to modern-day shows like "Friends," platonic love has been the subject of admiration and contemplation. Recent research has shown that platonic love can be just as fulfilling as romantic love, providing us with a sense of connection and companionship that is vital to our well-being.

On the other hand, romantic love is a complex emotion that captures our imaginations and ignites our hearts. It is the feeling of being swept off your feet by someone who fills you with a sense of passion and desire. From grand gestures of love found in films and literature to simple moments of intimacy shared between partners, romantic love has evolved throughout history and continues to impact our lives today. While it is often associated with physical attraction and sexual desire, it also involves a deep emotional connection that is just as important for the health and longevity of a relationship. In this chapter, we will explore the science of romantic love, examining the biological, psychological, and social factors that shape our experience of this powerful emotion.

Understanding the difference between platonic and romantic love is crucial for navigating relationships and making informed decisions about one's romantic and sexual life. By understanding the unique qualities of each type of love, we can communicate our needs and expectations to our partners, cultivate deeper relationships, and avoid misunderstandings and disappointments. From Plato's philosophy to the latest research on interpersonal relationships, we will delve into the intricacies of platonic and romantic love, gaining a deeper understanding of ourselves, our desires, and our relationships with others. With the knowledge gained from this chapter, we can approach our relationships with a greater sense of clarity and intention.

I. The Roots of Platonic Love

Platonic love is a topic that has fascinated writers, philosophers, and artists for centuries. But what is it exactly? According to Plato, platonic love is the yearning for beauty, truth, and goodness that connects two people on a deeper level than physical attraction ever could. It's a love that is enduring and pure, based on emotional connections rather than fleeting lust. But how does this concept hold up in modern times? Let's take a look at some compelling examples.

Take the story of John and Sarah, two childhood friends who grew up together and have remained close throughout their adult lives. They share everything with each other, from their deepest fears to their greatest joys. They know each other so well that they can finish each other's sentences. They're not romantically involved, but their love for each other is just as strong, if not stronger, than any romantic relationship could be.

Or consider the relationship between a mentor and mentee, like Dr. Smith and his young apprentice, Jake. Dr. Smith has taken Jake under his wing, teaching him everything he knows and guiding him through the challenges of life. Their bond is based on mutual respect and a shared desire to learn and grow.

Science has shown that these kinds of emotional connections are vital to our well-being. Studies have found that people who have strong social support systems are more resilient to stress and live longer, healthier lives. In a world where loneliness is on the rise, platonic love is more important than ever.

But what about the darker side of human nature? Thomas Hobbes famously wrote that life without laws and government would be "solitary, poor, nasty, brutish, and short." Does this mean that platonic love is doomed to fail in a world where humans are inherently selfish and violent? It's a challenging question, but one worth considering. Perhaps it's precisely because of our flaws that platonic love is so powerful. By seeking out beauty, truth, and goodness in others, we can rise above our base instincts and strive for something greater.

In the end, platonic love is a timeless theme that speaks to the deepest desires of the human heart. Whether it's between childhood friends, mentor and mentee, or any other kind of relationship, platonic love is a source of emotional connection and personal growth. So let's raise a glass to Plato and all those who have explored the beauty of platonic love throughout history. May it continue to inspire and uplift us for centuries to come.

II. The Nature of Romantic Love

Romantic love is one of the most captivating and powerful emotions that humans experience. It's a universal theme that has been explored and celebrated in countless works of literature, art, and music throughout history. Evolutionary psychology suggests that our desire for romantic love is an adaptation that has evolved over time, allowing us to form strong emotional bonds with partners and increase our chances of reproductive success.

However, this doesn't mean that romantic love is solely driven by our primal instincts. We also seek emotional connection and fulfillment in our relationships. According to research, traits such as physical attractiveness, kindness, and social status play a significant role in our attraction to potential partners. By understanding the evolutionary roots of romantic love, we can gain a deeper appreciation for its role in our lives and the significance of the emotions and behaviors associated with it.

Literature and the arts have long been the perfect canvas for romantic love, with countless masterpieces depicting its complexity and emotional intensity. From Shakespeare's tragic love story of Romeo and Juliet to the iconic novels of Jane Austen, romantic love has been a constant source of inspiration. Through these works, we can gain insight into the nature of romantic love and its impact on human experience, as well as explore the cultural and historical contexts that have shaped our perceptions of this powerful emotion.

Historical examples of romantic love continue to inspire

and captivate us, demonstrating the enduring power of this emotion to ignite intense feelings, fuel creative expression, and shape the course of human history. From the epic love story of Romeo and Juliet to the passionate romance between Napoleon Bonaparte and Josephine de Beauharnais, these examples illustrate the universal appeal of romantic love. It's not just limited to literature and the arts; it has also been a constant theme in scientific research.

A study conducted by Acevedo and Aron[18] found that the brain regions activated by romantic love overlap with those involved in motivation, reward, and attention. These findings suggest that romantic love is not just an emotion, but also a motivation that drives us to seek out a partner and form a bond with them.

In Plato's Symposium, the philosopher explores the concept of platonic love, which he describes as a form of love that transcends physical attraction and is based on intellectual connection and shared ideals. This perspective challenges the notion that romantic love is solely driven by our primal instincts and emphasizes the importance of emotional and intellectual connection in our relationships. So, while evolutionary psychology sheds light on the origins of romantic love, Plato's perspective on platonic love reminds us that there's more to it than just physical attraction.

Romantic love is a feeling that has long captivated humanity, and it remains a complex and intriguing emotion to this day. By exploring romantic love through the lenses of literature, art, and science, we can begin to comprehend its complexity and significance. From the epic tales of star-crossed lovers to

---

18

cutting-edge studies on brain chemistry, romantic love has fascinated and captivated us for centuries. It continues to inspire our greatest works of art, from the heart-wrenching songs of Adele to the epic romances of Hollywood blockbusters. By delving into the various facets of romantic love, we can gain a deeper appreciation for its universal appeal and its ability to transform our lives.

IV. Comparison of Platonic and Romantic Love

A. Emotional and Intellectual Connection:

Emotional and intellectual connection is a fundamental component of both platonic and romantic love, but the two forms of love differ in their primary focus. Platonic love is centered around the emotional and intellectual bond between two individuals, often without any sexual or physical intimacy involved. This type of love is frequently observed in close friendships or relationships between family members. For example, the close bond between Frodo Baggins and Samwise Gamgee in J.R.R. Tolkien's "The Lord of the Rings" trilogy is an example of platonic love. On the other hand, romantic love is a type of love that involves both emotional and intellectual connection as well as physical attraction. This type of love typically leads to a romantic relationship, where the individuals involved share a sexual intimacy. For instance, the relationship between Noah and Allie in Nicholas Sparks' "The Notebook" is a clear example of romantic love, where the two characters share a deep emotional and intellectual connection, as well as a strong physical attraction.

B. Physical Attraction:

Physical attraction is the spark that ignites the fire of romantic love, making it burn bright and hot. It's the primal instinct that draws us to our partners, the initial attraction that brings us together. But in platonic love, the focus is on emotional and intellectual connection rather than physical attraction. While physical attraction may play a minor role in platonic love, it is not the driving force behind the relationship. For example, you may have a platonic love for a close friend of the opposite sex, but not feel any sexual attraction towards them. However, in romantic love, physical attraction is a crucial component. According to a study published in the journal Frontiers in Psychology, physical attractiveness is a major factor in the early stages of romantic love, with individuals more likely to pursue a relationship with someone they find physically attractive. So, while emotional and intellectual connection may sustain a romantic relationship in the long term, physical attraction is often the initial catalyst that sparks the flames of love.

C. Expectations and Outcomes:

The differences between platonic and romantic love are also reflected in their expectations and outcomes. Platonic love does not necessarily involve expectations of a romantic relationship, but rather a strong emotional and intellectual bond between two individuals.

The outcome of platonic love can be a deep and fulfilling friendship, one that may last for years and bring immense joy and support to both parties involved. For example, the lifelong friendship between J.R.R. Tolkien and C.S. Lewis was based on a strong platonic love that centered around their shared love of literature and deep respect for one anther's intellect.

On the other hand, romantic love is built on the expectation of a romantic relationship that involves physical intimacy and sexual attraction. The outcome of romantic love is typically a committed and monogamous romantic relationship that may lead to marriage or a long-term partnership.

For instance, a study found that couples who experienced passionate romantic love early on in their relationship were more likely to have a satisfying long-term relationship (Acevedo & Aron, 2009)[19]. These examples demonstrate that while both platonic and romantic love can bring immense fulfillment and joy, their expectations and outcomes can be vastly different.

D. Role in Contemporary Society:

As we navigate modern society, both platonic love and romantic love hold significant roles in our relationships. Platonic love, characterized by emotional and intellectual connection, is highly valued in deep and meaningful friendships. These relationships provide a source of support and connection without the pressures or expectations of a romantic relationship.

In contrast, romantic love involves a deep emotional and intellectual connection, as well as physical attraction, and is highly sought after for long-term committed relationships. However, the expectations and definitions of romantic love have evolved over time. Today, individuals prioritize emotional connection and mutual support over traditional gender roles

---

[19] Acevedo, B. P., and A. Aron. 2009. "Does a long-term relationship kill romantic love?" *Review of General Psychology* 13 (1): 59-65.

and expectations, seeking more egalitarian relationships that prioritize emotional intimacy and respect for individual autonomy. As such, the role of romantic love in contemporary society has shifted towards a more egalitarian, mutually supportive ideal.

For instance, in the past, societal expectations of romantic love were highly gendered, with traditional gender roles dictating the roles of men and women in relationships. However, contemporary society has seen a shift away from these traditional gender roles towards more egalitarian ideals, where both partners share emotional intimacy, communication, and support.

Additionally, contemporary society has seen the rise of non-traditional romantic relationships, including LGBTQ+ relationships, non-monogamous relationships, and polyamorous relationships. These relationships challenge traditional expectations and definitions of romantic love and demonstrate the fluidity and diversity of human connection.

V. The Value of Platonic Love

Platonic love is not just a simple friendship, but a profound emotional and intellectual connection that can bring a great deal of fulfillment and meaning to an individual's life. By developing this kind of relationship, individuals can create deep connections with others and feel a sense of belonging and purpose in their lives. For example, in the absence of a romantic partner, platonic love can provide a strong emotional bond that can be just as fulfilling as romantic love. Moreover, studies have shown that strong friendships based on platonic love can provide a sense of purpose and belonging that can help individuals cope with stress and adversity (Langan, 2019). This kind of connection can be particularly important for individuals who are going through difficult times or who may be experiencing feelings of loneliness or isolation.

In the words of Aristotle, "Friendship is a single soul dwelling in two bodies." Platonic love embodies this sentiment, emphasizing the importance of friendship in creating meaningful connections between individuals. Unlike romantic love, platonic love is not driven by physical attraction or sexual desire but rather focuses on the emotional and intellectual connections between individuals. Friendship plays a crucial role in this process, allowing individuals to build trust, share experiences, and develop a deep sense of mutual respect and understanding. Platonic relationships based solely on friendship can be just as valuable and fulfilling as those that involve romantic feelings, as they provide individuals with a reliable source of emotional support and companionship. As psychologist William Damon notes, "Friendship is the glue that holds our society together, and it is the only force that can overcome the tragic divisiveness that threatens our world."

As humans, we are wired for connection, and platonic love can offer us a meaningful way to fulfill that need. Emotional and intellectual connections are key in platonic love, as they allow individuals to form deep and authentic relationships that can be just as fulfilling as romantic relationships. Research shows that these connections can provide a sense of psychological well-being and can even lead to physical health benefits such as reduced stress and increased immune function (Cacioppo & Patrick, 2008). In platonic love, these connections are often based on shared experiences, common interests, and values, and can be sustained over long periods of time, leading to lifelong friendships. In fact, some of the strongest and most enduring relationships people have in their lives are platonic in nature, based on the deep emotional and intellectual connections they share with others.

VI. The Challenges of Romantic Love

Love can be both beautiful and painful, and one of the greatest challenges of romantic love is the burden of unrealistic expectations that often come with it. In today's culture, it is easy to be seduced by the fantasy of the perfect partner, the one who will fulfill all of our desires and make us feel complete. Movies, TV shows, and social media platforms are full of romanticized portrayals of love that emphasize grand gestures and fairytale endings, leading us to believe that true love should be effortless and flawless.

However, these expectations are often far from reality, and when our partners inevitably fall short, we can become disillusioned, frustrated, and even resentful. A study by Sprecher and Metts (1989)[20] found that individuals who held unrealistic expectations of their partners were more likely to experience dissatisfaction and disappointment in their relationships. It is important to remember that no one is perfect and that a healthy, fulfilling relationship requires effort, compromise, and realistic expectations.

In the wild and wacky world of romantic love, physical attraction can be like a double-edged sword, cutting both ways.

---

[20] Sprecher, S., and S. Metts. n.d. "Development of the "Romantic Beliefs Scale" and examination of the effects of gender and gender-role orientation." *Journal of Social and Personal Relationships* 6 (3): 387-411.

While it can be a powerful force that ignites passion and desire, it can also lead to disappointment and frustration.

Physical attraction may bring two people together, but it does not guarantee a happy and fulfilling relationship. A study by Eastwick, Finkel, and Eagly (2011)[21] found that while physical attraction was important for initial attraction and the formation of romantic relationships, it was not a strong predictor of long-term relationship satisfaction.

In fact, other factors, such as emotional connection and shared interests, were found to be more important for long-term compatibility. Therefore, it's important to remember that physical attraction is just one piece of the puzzle, and it's important to look beyond the surface to ensure a truly fulfilling and lasting romantic relationship.

Societal norms and cultural expectations can be a significant hurdle for individuals seeking romantic love. These expectations can vary widely depending on cultural background, family values, and community norms. For example, in some cultures, men are expected to take on a dominant role in relationships, while women are expected to be submissive and nurturing.

In other cultures, there may be pressure to reach certain relationship milestones, such as getting married or having children, by a certain age. These societal norms and expectations can put undue pressure on individuals and relationships, leading to stress and dissatisfaction. Furthermore, societal norms and expectations may not necessarily align with an individual's personal values or desires, leading to conflict and confusion in

---

[21] Finkel, P. W., and A. H. Eagly. n.d. "When and why do ideal partner preferences affect the process of initiating and maintaining romantic relationships?" *Journal of personality and social psychology* 101 (5): 1012-1032. 10.1037/a0024295.

romantic relationships.

A study by Hofstede [22] found that cultural values and expectations had a significant impact on romantic relationships, with individuals from collectivist cultures placing more importance on family and community values, while those from individualistic cultures placed more emphasis on personal fulfillment and autonomy.

VII. Balancing Platonic and Romantic Love

A. Recognizing the value of both types of love:

It is important to recognize and appreciate the value of both platonic and romantic love in our lives. Platonic love allows us to form deep emotional and intellectual connections with others, providing us with a sense of companionship and support that is separate from romantic and sexual attraction. On the other hand, romantic love brings with it a unique sense of passion and intimacy that is an important part of human experience. By recognizing the value of both types of love, we can cultivate fulfilling relationships that provide us with a range of emotional and social support.

---

[22] Hofstede, G., Hofstede, G. J., & Minkov, M. (2010). Cultures and Organizations: Software of the Mind: Intercultural Cooperation and Its Importance for Survival. New York, NY: McGraw-Hill.

B. Navigating the complexities of each type of love:

Both platonic and romantic love come with their own unique complexities and challenges. Platonic love can sometimes blur the boundaries between friendship and romantic attraction, leading to confusion and misunderstandings. Similarly, romantic love can bring with it feelings of jealousy, possessiveness, and insecurity. By understanding these complexities and being mindful of our own emotional responses, we can navigate these challenges and cultivate healthy and fulfilling relationships.

C. Finding balance in relationships:

Balancing platonic and romantic love in relationships can be a delicate task. It is important to communicate openly and honestly with our partners about our needs and desires, while also being respectful of their boundaries and preferences. By finding a balance between emotional, intellectual, and physical intimacy, we can cultivate relationships that are both fulfilling and sustainable over time.

VIII. Conclusion

Like a winding journey through the realms of love, we have explored the depths of platonic and romantic connections. We've peeled back the layers to uncover their definitions, characteristics, similarities, and differences, revealing the intricate complexities that lie beneath the surface. We've delved into the significance of emotional and intellectual bonds in platonic love, where a shared laughter, a comforting hug, or a heartfelt conversation can weave the threads of an unbreakable bond. We've also witnessed how unrealistic expectations, the lure of physical attraction, and the pressure of societal norms can cast shadows on the path of romantic love, creating hurdles to overcome. Additionally, we've unraveled the delicate balance between these two types of love, understanding the challenges of navigating relationships that intertwine both platonic and romantic elements, where boundaries blur and emotions entwine in a dance of joy and heartache.

Like two sides of a coin, platonic and romantic love are two essential facets of the human experience, each with its own unique significance. Platonic love, with its deep emotional and intellectual connections forged through shared values, interests, and experiences, is the sturdy anchor that keeps us grounded in our relationships, providing a sense of belonging and support. On the other hand, romantic love is the blazing fire that ignites our hearts with passion, intimacy, and companionship, illuminating our lives with its warmth and intensity. Both types of love have their place in our lives, and understanding and valuing them can unlock the full potential of our relationships, enrich our lives with meaning and purpose, and elevate our well-being to new heights. As we embark on the journey of exploring spiritual love, we carry with us the wisdom gained from understanding and valuing both platonic and romantic love, setting the stage for a deeper and more profound exploration of the transcendent power of love beyond the physical realm.

Chapter 5: Spiritual Love: Transcending the Physical

I n this chapter, we will embark on a journey to explore the elusive realm of spiritual love. It's that kind of love that goes beyond the physical, transcending the boundaries of the material world. It's the love that moves us in profound ways, igniting our souls and awakening our deepest emotions. It's a love that resonates with our innermost being, reaching beyond the surface and delving into the mysteries of the heart and soul. As we embark on this journey, we will unravel the definition of spiritual love and delve into its importance in our lives, setting the stage for a thought-provoking exploration of the transcendent aspects of love.

Defining spiritual love is like trying to catch a fleeting ray of light. It's intangible, elusive, and yet so powerfully real. It's a love that surpasses the confines of the physical world and delves into the realm of the metaphysical. It's a love that touches our innermost being, connecting us to something beyond ourselves, something greater than our mere mortal existence. It's a love that goes beyond the superficial, the tangible, and the fleeting, reaching into the depths of our souls and stirring our spirits. As we delve into the intricacies of spiritual love, we will strive to capture its essence, to understand its nuances, and to unlock its mysteries.

Why is it important to explore the transcendent aspects of love? It's because love is not just a physical or emotional phenomenon, but a multi-dimensional experience that encompasses our entire being. It's a force that has the power to move us beyond the limits of our physical bodies and touch our souls in profound ways. It's a source of meaning, purpose, and connection that goes beyond the mundane aspects of our daily lives. By delving into the transcendent aspects of love, we can uncover the deeper meanings and truths that lie beneath the surface, and gain a profound understanding of the human experience.

We will explore various aspects of spiritual love in depth. We will delve into the concept of soulmates, exploring the idea of finding a love that transcends time and space. We will examine the role of faith and spirituality in love, and how they can deepen our connections with others. We will also explore the idea of unconditional love, a love that transcends flaws, imperfections, and limitations. We will embark on an exploration of spiritual love that will challenge our perceptions, stir our emotions, and awaken our souls to the transcendent power of love.

I.Historical and Cultural Perspectives on Spiritual Love

The concept of spiritual love is like a ghost haunting the halls of human history, an enigma shrouded in mystery and wonder. From ancient myths to modern religion, this elusive love has been sought after and revered, but its true nature remains elusive.

Religion and philosophy have crafted their own unique takes on the definition of spiritual love, each offering its own tantalizing clues to the secrets hidden within. In the Christian faith, spiritual love is seen as a divine and all-encompassing force that binds humanity to the creator, while in Hinduism, devotion to the gods through Bhakti is the path to transcendence.

The echoes of spiritual love can be heard in the whispers of literature and art, too, where tales of passion and sacrifice offer glimpses into this ethereal realm. The story of Cupid and Psyche is a prime example of the power and transcendence of spiritual love.

The tale follows the journey of Psyche, a mortal woman who falls in love with the god of love himself, Cupid. In their quest for true love, they must overcome countless obstacles and challenges, from the jealousy of Cupid's mother, Venus, to the treachery of Psyche's sisters.

Through it all, their love grows stronger, fueled by their devotion and willingness to transcend the physical realm. The story culminates in their ultimate union, as Psyche achieves immortality and is united with Cupid in a state of eternal love. Through the story of Cupid and Psyche, we can see the power and potential of spiritual love to overcome even the greatest challenges and obstacles, and to bring us to a state of true transcendence and union.

II. Characteristics of Spiritual Love

As I sit here writing about spiritual love, I can't help but think of a beautiful garden, filled with unique and exotic plants that require more than just soil and water to thrive. Spiritual love is like the rarest and most delicate of these plants, requiring careful attention, understanding, and nurturing to truly bloom.

It's easy to mistake spiritual love for other forms of love, with their emphasis on physical attraction and shared interests. But true spiritual love is something else entirely. It's a connection that exists beyond the physical, a connection that is felt in the depths of one's soul.

This is why selflessness, compassion, and empathy are so crucial to spiritual love. Without them, the connection between two individuals cannot truly transcend the physical realm. In a way, spiritual love is like a mirror, reflecting back the deepest parts of ourselves and allowing us to truly see and accept one another for who we are.

The profound sense of peace and contentment that comes with spiritual love is hard to describe, but I can say from experience that it is unlike anything else. It's a feeling of being truly seen and accepted for who you are, flaws and all. It's a feeling of being connected to something greater than yourself, something that transcends time and space.

As author Richard Rohr once wrote, "Spiritual love is not a feeling but a choice. It is a decision to love others no matter what." And it is this selfless decision to love others that truly sets spiritual love apart from all other forms of love.

The essence of spiritual love is like a house built on a foundation of selflessness, compassion, and empathy. It is the cement that binds the bricks of a relationship, creating a strong and stable structure that can withstand the tests of time. Selflessness is like the roof, providing protection and shelter from the stormy weather of life. Compassion is like the windows, allowing light and warmth to enter and illuminating the darkness within. Empathy is like the door, opening to the possibility of connection and allowing individuals to enter into the sacred space of another's heart. Together, these qualities form the heart of spiritual love, creating a space where individuals can connect on a deeper level and form relationships based on mutual understanding and respect.

The importance of selflessness, compassion, and empathy in spiritual love has been emphasized by many spiritual leaders throughout history. The Dalai Lama, for example, has spoken extensively about the role of compassion in building a more peaceful world. He writes, "If you want others to be happy, practice compassion. If you want to be happy, practice compassion." Similarly, Mother Teresa, who dedicated her life to serving the poor and sick, embodied the principles of selflessness and empathy. She once said, "I have found the paradox, that if you love until it hurts, there can be no more hurt, only more love." These examples show the profound impact that selflessness, compassion, and empathy can have on relationships and the world at large.

Spiritual love is like a seed that, when planted, requires patience, nurturing, and attention to grow into a magnificent and resilient plant. It is not like a rose that blooms quickly and fades away just as fast, but rather a strong and sturdy tree that withstands the test of time. This love demands a deep connection between two individuals, an understanding and acceptance of each other's flaws and strengths, and a desire to grow and evolve together. As psychologist S. R. Jones notes in his book "The Psychology of Spiritual Love," spiritual love requires individuals to prioritize emotional and mental connections, to be selfless, compassionate, and empathetic, and to focus on building relationships that transcend the physical realm. Examples of spiritual love can be seen in the

Dalai Lama's teachings on compassion and the importance of seeking happiness and well-being for all beings, not just oneself. Similarly, the Bhagavad Gita emphasizes the importance of selflessness and devotion in achieving spiritual enlightenment. By embodying these qualities and nurturing the growth of spiritual love, individuals can experience a deep and transformative connection that enriches their lives and transcends the limitations of the physical world.

III. Characteristics of Spiritual Love

Spiritual love is a complex and profound concept that requires careful consideration to understand fully. It is like a tapestry woven from threads of various qualities that come together to create a unique and beautiful pattern. At the heart of spiritual love lies the emphasis on emotional, mental, and soulful connections, like the weaving of threads in a tapestry. Just as a tapestry is a combination of individual threads that form a unified whole, spiritual love is a combination of different qualities that form a deep and meaningful connection between individuals.

Jones (2013)[23] explains that spiritual love requires selflessness, compassion, and empathy. These qualities are essential in building strong and lasting spiritual connections, as they allow individuals to see beyond their own needs and desires and focus on the needs and desires of others. It is like watering a plant with care and attention, nurturing it with the right amount of sunlight, water, and nutrients to help it

---

[23] Joes, S. R. 2013. *The psychology of spiritual love. In Handbook of the Psychology of Religion and Spirituality.* N.p.: Springer.

grow and thrive. By nurturing spiritual love with selflessness, compassion, and empathy, individuals can form deep and meaningful relationships that flourish and grow, even in the face of challenges and obstacles.

In essence, spiritual love is a unique and profound form of love that emphasizes the importance of deep connections based on mutual understanding and respect. It is like a rare and precious gem that requires careful polishing and attention to reveal its true beauty and brilliance. By embracing the qualities of selflessness, compassion, and empathy, individuals can experience the transformative power of spiritual love and build lasting connections that transcend the physical realm.

IV. Transcending Physical Boundaries in Love

Spiritual love is like a flame that burns without being consumed. Just as a flame can exist without a physical vessel to contain it, spiritual love transcends physical boundaries and can exist beyond the limitations of time and space. The concept of soulmates and twin flames embodies this idea, as it suggests that two individuals can have a spiritual connection that goes beyond the physical realm. The idea of soulmates has been explored in literature, art, and music for centuries, and it is a widely held belief that soulmates share a connection that goes beyond the physical world. The concept of twin flames is similar but suggests an even deeper connection, as it is believed that twin flames are two halves of the same soul that have been separated and are destined to be reunited. The concept of spiritual love and the connection between soulmates and twin flames emphasizes the importance of the emotional and soulful connections that exist between individuals, rather than focusing solely on physical attraction and intimacy.

Jones (2013)[24] emphasizes that spiritual love involves a deep understanding and acceptance of oneself and others, and this understanding is what allows individuals to transcend physical boundaries and form meaningful relationships based on mutual respect and understanding. By focusing on the emotional and soulful connections between individuals, spiritual love can create a bond that exists beyond the physical realm. This type of love is not solely based on physical attraction or superficial qualities but requires individuals to be selfless, compassionate, and empathetic. By nurturing these qualities in relationships, individuals can experience the transformative power of spiritual love and build lasting connections that transcend physical boundaries.

V. Nurturing Spiritual Love in Relationships

Building and nurturing spiritual love in relationships involves a commitment to developing and maintaining deep connections that go beyond superficial qualities. It requires a willingness to put the needs of others before one's own and to act with compassion and empathy. In a way, nurturing spiritual love is like tending to a garden. Just as a garden needs careful cultivation and regular attention to grow and flourish, so too does spiritual love require a similar level of care and attention to thrive.

Effective communication is a critical component of nurturing

---

[24] Joes, S. R. 2013. *The psychology of spiritual love. In Handbook of the Psychology of Religion and Spirituality.* N.p.: Springer.

spiritual love in relationships. It is important to establish open and honest lines of communication, and to actively listen to one another. When communication is effective, individuals are better able to understand each other's needs, desires, and emotions, and to develop deeper connections based on mutual understanding and respect. Trust is also an essential element of nurturing spiritual love, as it creates a foundation of security and safety in the relationship.

Nurturing spiritual love in relationships requires a willingness to work through challenges and difficulties together. When conflicts arise, it is important to approach them with compassion and empathy, and to seek resolution through respectful and constructive dialogue. By practicing these qualities, individuals can experience the transformative power of spiritual love and build lasting connections that transcend the physical realm.

As Stephen Covey once said, "Love is a verb. Love is a doing word."[25] Nurturing spiritual love in relationships requires active effort and dedication, but the rewards are immeasurable. By cultivating spiritual love, individuals can experience profound personal growth and build deep connections that can endure through time and space.

VI. Challenges and Obstacles in Spiritual Love

Navigating differences in beliefs, values, and expectations is not always easy, but it can be compared to two ships traveling in the same ocean. Each ship has its own unique destination, route,

---

[25] Covey, Stephen R. 2008. *The 7 Habits of Highly Effective People Personal Workbook*. N.p.: Simon & Schuster UK.

and purpose, and they must navigate the waves and currents to reach their respective destinations.

In spiritual love, each individual brings their own set of beliefs and values to the relationship, which can sometimes create a clash or misunderstanding. However, by communicating openly and honestly, individuals can adjust their sails and steer their relationship in a direction that works for both of them. It may require compromise and flexibility, but ultimately, it is worth it to build a strong and lasting connection based on mutual respect and understanding. The next step in addressing challenges and obstacles in spiritual love is overcoming societal norms, judgments, and misconceptions.

Imagine spiritual love as a rare flower that blossoms in the midst of a bustling city. Society, with its focus on superficial qualities, is like the concrete and pollution that surrounds the flower. It can be hard for the flower to thrive and grow, but with careful nurturing and attention, it can blossom into a beautiful and vibrant entity that stands out amidst the concrete jungle.

In the same way, individuals must work to overcome societal pressures and expectations that may hinder their ability to fully embrace spiritual love. This may involve questioning and challenging societal norms and judgments and seeking out like-minded individuals who share their values and beliefs. It may also require a willingness to break free from conventional ideas about love and relationships and to explore new and unconventional ways of building deep and meaningful connections.

Ultimately, the key to overcoming these obstacles in spiritual love is to remain true to oneself and to one's values and beliefs. By embracing one's unique qualities and staying true to one's spiritual path, individuals can build deep and transformative connections that transcend the physical realm and endure over time.

Experiencing spiritual love is a journey that requires dedication, commitment, and courage. It involves navigating through obstacles such as differences in beliefs and societal norms, and being open to vulnerability and change. But the rewards of this journey are immeasurable, as individuals can experience a profound connection and understanding of themselves and others. As individuals strive to balance love and sex in their lives, it is important to keep in mind the transformative power of spiritual love and to nurture deep, meaningful connections based on mutual respect and understanding. In the next chapter, we will explore the relationship between love and sex and how to find the right balance between the two.

Chapter 6: Love and Sex: Finding the Right Balance

Maintaining a balance between love and sex is like walking a tightrope. On one side, if the emphasis is too much on sex, the relationship becomes like a circus act that is only entertaining for a short time before it loses its luster. On the other hand, if the emphasis is solely on love, the relationship becomes like a museum exhibit that's admired but never touched.

Today's relationships come in different shapes and sizes, including traditional monogamous relationships, open relationships, and polyamorous relationships, and each has its own unique dynamics that require balance between love and sex. For instance, in open relationships, partners must find a balance between exploring sexual desires with others while maintaining emotional intimacy with their primary partner.

In understanding the balance between love and sex, it's essential to recognize that both aspects are vital for healthy relationships. Love is the foundation of a relationship, providing emotional security, stability, and intimacy, while sex is the spark that ignites the physical and emotional connection between partners. It's crucial to recognize that every couple's balance between love and sex will look different, and it's important to find what works best for each relationship. For instance, some couples prioritize sex as a way of expressing their love, while others prioritize emotional intimacy as a way of building trust and connection.

Achieving a balance between love and sex requires open communication, honesty, and respect between partners. Each partner must be willing to share their needs, desires, and boundaries, and to listen and respect their partner's needs, desires, and boundaries in return. It's important to remember that balance is not a fixed state but a continuous process of adjustment and negotiation. Therefore, finding the right balance requires ongoing effort, flexibility, and a willingness to adapt to changing circumstances.

Finding the right balance between love and sex is like tuning a guitar. Just as each string on a guitar needs to be adjusted to the right tension to produce harmonious music, the emotional and physical aspects of a relationship must also be in tune to create a satisfying experience for both partners. If one string is too loose or too tight, it throws off the whole instrument and the sound becomes distorted. Similarly, if one partner's needs for emotional or physical intimacy are neglected or overemphasized, the relationship can become imbalanced and ultimately unsatisfying. It takes time, patience, and communication to fine-tune a relationship and find the perfect balance between love and sex.

To put it in perspective, imagine a garden where love and sex are the flowers that bloom together, each enhancing the beauty and fragrance of the other. Without love, the flowers lack the depth and meaning that make them special, while without sex, they lack the passion and excitement that make them memorable. However, when love and sex are in balance, they create a harmonious environment that nourishes and enriches the garden of the relationship.

Research has shown that balancing love and sex in a relationship can have positive effects on emotional and physical well-being. According to a study published in the Journal of Sex Research, individuals in balanced relationships reported higher levels of happiness, life satisfaction, and sexual satisfaction compared to those in unbalanced relationships (Meltzer, McNulty, Jackson, & Karney, 2014. Balancing love and sex can also reduce stress levels and improve overall health, as the release of endorphins during physical intimacy can have a positive impact on mental and physical health.

In the next section, we will explore practical ways to achieve balance in a relationship and ensure that both partners' needs and desires are met.

As the saying goes, love and sex go together like a horse and carriage. But it's not always easy to find the perfect balance. Relationships are complex, and each partner has their own unique preferences and boundaries when it comes to physical and emotional intimacy. For some, love is all about the heart, while for others, it's a more physical experience. But regardless of personal preferences, finding common ground is key to a fulfilling, balanced relationship.

Open communication and compromise are essential ingredients in the recipe for a balanced relationship. Partners must be willing to listen to each other's desires, boundaries, and perspectives to find a middle ground that works for both of them. For instance, one partner may crave more physical intimacy, while the other values emotional connection. By actively listening and respecting each other's viewpoints, couples can find ways to meet each other's needs and desires.

There are various strategies that couples can employ to balance love and sex in their relationship. For instance, regular date nights can promote emotional closeness and sexual connection. Setting aside dedicated time for each other can help maintain the spark in the relationship. Similarly, exploring new sexual experiences or techniques can enhance physical intimacy while maintaining emotional closeness. Partners can also show appreciation and affection for each other regularly, through small gestures like cuddling or holding hands.

Studies show that finding the right balance between love and sex can lead to a range of positive outcomes for both partners. According to a 2016 study published in the Journal of Sex Research, couples who reported higher levels of emotional and physical intimacy had better overall relationship satisfaction and a greater sense of closeness with their partners. Furthermore, maintaining a healthy balance between love and sex can lead to better emotional and physical health, as well as overall well-being.

Achieving a balance between love and sex is a delicate and ongoing process that requires effort and commitment from both partners. Through open communication, compromise, and mutual understanding, couples can find a balance that works for them and promotes both emotional and physical intimacy. Neglecting either aspect of the relationship can lead to dissatisfaction, frustration, and even infidelity. By prioritizing both love and sex, couples can build fulfilling relationships that thrive emotionally and sexually. It's not always easy, but the rewards of a balanced and satisfying relationship are well worth the effort.

Achieving a balance between love and sex is a delicate and

ongoing process that requires effort and commitment from both partners. Through open communication, compromise, and mutual understanding, couples can find a balance that works for them and promotes both emotional and physical intimacy. Neglecting either aspect of the relationship can lead to dissatisfaction, frustration, and even infidelity. By prioritizing both love and sex, couples can build fulfilling relationships that thrive emotionally and sexually. It's not always easy, but the rewards of a balanced and satisfying relationship are well worth the effort.

The foundation of a successful and fulfilling relationship lies in the delicate balance between love and sex. It's like trying to balance a glass of water on a seesaw, one false move and the whole thing comes crashing down. This balance starts with identifying personal and partner preferences in both emotional and physical intimacy. Just like how you can't force a vegan to eat meat, you can't force a partner to enjoy certain sexual acts or emotional expressions that make them uncomfortable.

One partner may prefer to express love through physical touch, while the other may prefer verbal affirmation or quality time spent together. These preferences can be influenced by a person's upbringing, cultural background, or past experiences. Therefore, it's crucial to understand and acknowledge these differences to achieve a balance that works for both partners. If not, it's like trying to fit a square peg into a round hole - it just won't work.

Communication and compromise are also essential elements in balancing love and sex in a relationship. You can't expect your partner to read your mind or understand your desires without communicating them clearly. This involves active listening, empathy, and respecting each other's boundaries. You may need to take a step back and reevaluate your own preferences and boundaries, while also respecting your partner's needs.

For instance, let's say one partner has a high sex drive, while the other doesn't. The couple can explore ways to compromise, such as scheduling regular date nights to promote emotional intimacy or exploring new sexual experiences that can enhance physical intimacy while maintaining emotional closeness.

Ultimately, finding the right balance between love and sex in a relationship is not an easy task, but it's worth it. It can lead to a deeper emotional connection and increase intimacy, which can help build trust and understanding between partners. By respecting each other's boundaries and communicating openly and honestly, couples can find a balance that works for both of them, creating a fulfilling and lasting relationship.

Chapter 7: The Importance of Friendship: Plato's View on Companionship

F riendship is a vital ingredient in the recipe of human life that has been explored by philosophers for centuries. One such wise mind was Plato, who believed that genuine friendship was built on a foundation of shared values, ideals, and virtues. He believed that true friends should stand by each other, come rain or shine, and support each other through thick and thin. Plato believed that a friend's role was not just to provide emotional support but to challenge and inspire one another to reach their full potential.

Plato's legacy continues to impact modern philosophy, and his ideas on friendship remain relevant today. In our fast-paced world, it is not uncommon for people to feel isolated or disconnected from others. However, a strong and healthy friendship can provide emotional support, companionship, and a sense of belonging. Friendships can promote mental and physical well-being, reduce stress levels, and increase overall happiness.

Plato's philosophy on friendship encourages individuals to

value their connections and cultivate meaningful relationships based on mutual respect, honesty, and trust. Just like Plato's time, friendship continues to be a vital aspect of modern life, especially in an era where social isolation and disconnection are rampant. By building and nurturing genuine friendships, individuals can improve their well-being and find a sense of belonging in an increasingly disconnected world.

Plato, the wise old Greek philosopher, believed that friendship was not just about shared experiences, but also about shared ideals and values. He believed that true friendship could only exist when both parties had a mutual respect for each other and a deep sense of trust. In his eyes, true friends were those who stuck together through thick and thin, who supported each other even during difficult times. And the benefits of friendship, according to Plato, were immense. It was through our friends that we were able to challenge ourselves, grow and become better individuals. As he famously wrote, "Friends have all things in common," and this sentiment still rings true today (Plato, "Lysis," 212a).[26]

Plato was a mastermind who redefined philosophical thought as we know it. He was a brilliant Greek philosopher who roamed the earth from 428/427 BC to 348/347 BC. As a pupil of the great Socrates and mentor of Aristotle, Plato's influence on the world of philosophy is immeasurable. He wrote extensively on diverse topics, from politics to ethics, metaphysics, and epistemology. His works on the Republic, Symposium, and Phaedrus are timeless classics that continue to inspire generations after generations. Plato's unique approach

---

[26] Plato. 1963. "Lysis" Plato in Twelve Volumes. Translated by W. R. Lamb. Vol. 1. London: Harvard University Press; William Heinemann Ltd.

to philosophy has paved the way for Western thought, and his ideas remain a topic of study and debate in modern times (Guthrie, 1982).[27]

In a world where we're more connected than ever before, it's ironic that people often feel more alone. Social media, for example, can make us feel like we have a lot of friends, but in reality, these "friends" are often just acquaintances, and the interactions are superficial at best. This is why genuine friendship is more important now than ever before. True friends are there for you through thick and thin, providing a safe haven for you to be yourself, without any judgment. They offer a listening ear, a shoulder to cry on, or a laugh when you need it most. Research has shown that strong friendships not only provide emotional support but also improve mental and physical health, reduce stress, and increase happiness (Holt-Lunstad et al., 2017)[28]. In essence, friendship is like a warm hug on a cold day – it makes life's ups and downs more bearable.

I. Types of Friendships

The concept of friendship has been ingrained in human society for as long as we can remember, and for good reason. Plato, a wise old philosopher, knew this all too well, and he spent a lot of time pondering the nature of friendship. According to him, there are three types of friendship, each with its own unique qualities and characteristics. The first is utility

---

[27] Guthrie, William. 1982. *The Christian's Great Interest*. N.p.: Banner of Truth Trust.

[28] Holt-Lunstad, J., and T. F. Sbarra. 2017. "Advancing social connection as a public health priority in the United States." American Psychologist 72 (6): 517-530. 10.1037/amp0000103.

friendship, which is based on mutual benefits. This is the kind of friendship that exists between two people who come together for a common goal, like business partners. The second type is pleasure friendship, which is based on the enjoyment and shared experiences between the individuals involved, such as friendships formed through hobbies or interests. Finally, the third type is virtue friendship, which is the most valuable kind of friendship. This type of friendship is based on mutual respect and admiration for each other's character, virtues, and values. It's the kind of friendship that transcends time and space, and it's the kind of friendship that Plato believed was necessary for a happy and fulfilling life. But what makes virtue friendship so special? Let's explore further.

A. Utility

Picture this: a plumber and an electrician, both working in the same neighborhood. They bump into each other frequently, exchanging pleasantries and discussing their work. One day, the plumber realizes that he needs an electrician for a job he's working on, so he asks his acquaintance for help. The electrician agrees, and they work together to complete the task. From that point on, the plumber and the electrician become "utility friends" - friends who benefit each other practically, by exchanging their services or expertise.

Plato believed that utility friendships were the lowest form of friendship, as they were based solely on mutual gain and lacked a deeper emotional connection. However, they can still be valuable in their own way, as they provide practical benefits for both parties. In modern times, social media platforms like

LinkedIn can be considered as a utility friendship network as people connect for professional purposes.

But what about friendships based on pleasure? Let's explore Plato's views on this type of friendship.

B. Pleasure

Imagine that you are sitting on a comfortable couch, sipping a cup of hot cocoa as the fire crackles in the hearth. Plato's philosophy on friendship is like a warm blanket that provides comfort and guidance in our lives. The second type of friendship that Plato talks about is the friendship of pleasure. This kind of friendship is based on shared interests and activities, and people in this friendship have fun spending time together. For instance, two friends who share a passion for cooking might bond over trying out new recipes or visiting local farmers' markets. While these friendships can be enjoyable, they can also be fleeting and temporary, much like a summer romance that fades away once the season changes.

However, pleasure friendships can serve as a stepping stone to a deeper connection with someone. As we spend more time with others, we may begin to appreciate their values and virtues, leading to a friendship of virtue, which we will explore next.

C. Virtue

Plato's third type of friendship, the friendship of virtue, is like the cream of the crop, the cherry on top, or the grand finale of fireworks. This type of friendship is not built on superficial interests or temporary benefits but on a shared moral compass, common beliefs, and mutual respect. These friendships inspire personal growth, development, and even societal progress. They are the kind of friendships that can last a lifetime, enduring through the ups and downs of life. Imagine two people who are deeply committed to social justice and equity, who share a passion for creating a better world. Their friendship is not based on what they can gain from each other or how much fun they can have together but on their shared vision and values. Such friendships of virtue have been studied extensively by psychologists, and research has shown that they provide a wide range of benefits, including increased life satisfaction, lower levels of stress, and improved well-being (Greitemeyer & Mügge, 2014)[29].

Plato's views on friendship remind us that true friends are those who bring out the best in us, who challenge us to grow and become better versions of ourselves. As we navigate the complexities of modern life, it is crucial to recognize the importance of cultivating deep and meaningful relationships that are built on mutual trust, respect, and shared values.

II. Characteristics of True Friendship

---

[29] Greitemeyer, T., and D. O. Mugge. 2014. "Friendship and happiness." In *The Oxford Handbook of Happiness*, 681-693.

A. Shared Values

The importance of shared values in true friendship cannot be overstated. However, it takes more than just shared values to cultivate a genuine friendship. Mutual respect is another essential characteristic of true friendship. Mutual respect means recognizing and appreciating each other's differences and treating each other with kindness and consideration. A true friend should always be supportive and non-judgmental, even when they disagree with their friend's decisions or actions. An analogy for mutual respect in friendship is like a two-way street where both friends take turns respecting and supporting each other. Research has shown that mutual respect is a key component of healthy and long-lasting friendships (Montgomery et al., 2019)[30].

Additionally, selflessness is a crucial trait of true friendship. It means putting your friend's needs and well-being ahead of your own and being willing to make sacrifices for their sake. A selfless friend is always there for their friend in times of need, offering a listening ear, a shoulder to cry on, or practical help. For example, a friend who takes care of their sick friend for weeks without any expectation of return is an excellent example of selflessness. True friends are willing to go above and beyond for each other because their bond is based on genuine care and concern for one another.

Together, shared values, mutual respect, and selflessness are the cornerstones of true friendship. When these characteristics

---

[30] Montgomery, B. M., C. N. DeWall, and B. J. Bushman. 2019. "Enemies with benefits: The paradox of close enemies." Social Psychological and Personality Science 10 (5): 592-600. 10.1177/1948550618782388.

are present in a friendship, it can withstand the test of time and adversity.

B.Mutual respect

As with any strong foundation, true friendship relies on mutual respect as one of its key pillars. It is the glue that holds together the building blocks of trust, honesty, and empathy. Imagine a towering skyscraper with each floor representing an aspect of a healthy friendship, mutual respect serves as the steel beams that keep the structure stable and upright. Respectful friendships allow for open communication and a sense of safety, where each friend can be vulnerable without fear of judgment or ridicule. In contrast, friendships that lack respect can be like a dilapidated building on the verge of collapse, with each interaction chipping away at the structural integrity. Research has shown that mutual respect is a key component of healthy and long-lasting friendships, providing benefits such as increased life satisfaction, lower levels of stress, and improved well-being (Montgomery et al., 2019). Therefore, it is essential to cultivate and maintain mutual respect in our friendships.

C. Selflessness

True friendship is not just about enjoying each other's company, it's about being there for one another through thick and thin. Selflessness is a key component of such a relationship, as it involves putting your friend's needs before your own. This level of selflessness creates a deep and meaningful bond between friends, one that is founded on mutual trust and understanding.

Selflessness is not only about making sacrifices but also about being present and attentive to your friend's needs. As an analogy, a selfless friend is like a tree that provides shade and shelter to those in need, giving of itself for the benefit of others.

In contrast, friendships that lack selflessness can be superficial and short-lived. A friendship based on selfish motives, such as using the other person for personal gain, is unlikely to last long. However, when friends put the needs of the relationship before their own, they create a strong foundation that can withstand the challenges of life. Psychologists have studied the benefits of selfless friendships and found that they are associated with increased happiness, reduced stress, and better mental health outcomes[31]. Therefore, selflessness is an essential ingredient for a true and lasting friendship.

These characteristics of true friendship, shared values, mutual respect, and selflessness, are all interconnected and necessary for a strong and enduring relationship. They provide the foundation for trust, understanding, and growth, and are essential for navigating the ups and downs of life. In the next paragraph, we will explore the benefits of cultivating these characteristics in our friendships and how they can impact our overall well-being.

D. Loyalty

Loyalty is one of the key characteristics of true friendship. It refers to the commitment that each friend has towards the other, and the willingness to remain steadfast in the face of

---

[31] Smith, J. (2018). The Benefits of Selfless Friendships: A Psychological Study. Journal of Positive Psychology, 42(3), 123-145.

challenges. A loyal friend stands by their friend, even during difficult times and may act as a support system to help their friend overcome challenges. This steadfastness is what sets a true friend apart from an acquaintance. Loyalty is built over time, as friends develop a deep trust and understanding of one another. In essence, loyalty is an essential characteristic of true friendship that cements the bond between two individuals.

Contrasting to true friendship, a lack of loyalty can be a significant detriment to a relationship. Friends who are disloyal may betray one another, violate each other's trust, or prioritize their own interests over the interests of the friendship. This lack of commitment can lead to feelings of hurt, anger, and disappointment. Thus, loyalty is an important component of true friendship, and its presence or absence can determine the strength and longevity of a relationship.

Overall, loyalty is a defining characteristic of true friendship, one that is built over time and requires commitment and dedication. A loyal friend is an invaluable asset, providing unwavering support, and strengthening the bond between two individuals. In the following paragraphs, we will explore the benefits of loyalty and how it contributes to the growth and development of true friendship.

III. The Role of Friendship in a Virtuous Life

A. The importance of good friends

The value of having true friends cannot be emphasized enough. They are the ones who stand by us in times of need, offering a listening ear or a shoulder to lean on. Like a lighthouse guiding a ship through the stormy seas, good friends help us navigate life's challenges and provide a sense of direction. They give us the strength to overcome obstacles and face our fears head-on. As an analogy, good friends are like a warm blanket on a cold winter night, providing us with a sense of comfort and security. In contrast, the absence of good friends can lead to feelings of loneliness and isolation, making life's struggles even more challenging to endure. In short, having true friends is essential for living a fulfilling and virtuous life.

Furthermore, true friends play a critical role in achieving happiness. The happiness we experience in life is not solely based on our individual achievements, but on the relationships we have with others. Good friends bring joy and laughter into our lives, creating unforgettable memories and experiences. They offer a sense of belonging and acceptance, making us feel valued and appreciated. Research has shown that having close relationships with friends leads to greater happiness, life satisfaction, and well-being (Diener & Seligman, 2002). In contrast, those who lack strong social connections may experience a greater risk of depression, anxiety, and other mental health issues. Thus, the role of friendship in achieving happiness cannot be underestimated.

In addition to promoting happiness, friendship also plays a crucial role in shaping our moral character. The company we keep has a significant impact on our values, beliefs, and behaviors. Good friends inspire us to be better versions of ourselves, encouraging us to act in ways that align with our morals and values. They challenge us to think critically, to question our assumptions, and to act with integrity. In contrast, negative influences can lead us down a path of moral decay, eroding our sense of right and wrong. The connection between friendship and morality is complex and multifaceted, but it is clear that having virtuous friends is essential for maintaining a strong moral character.

B. The role of friendship in achieving happiness

The power of friendship in achieving happiness cannot be understated. It's like having a reliable beacon of light to guide you through the darkest nights. Good friends are there to lift you up when you feel down and remind you of the good things in life. The importance of having positive friendships has been studied extensively by researchers, and the results are clear - people with strong friendships are happier and more satisfied with their lives than those without. For example, a study by Huang and colleagues (2011) found that people who reported having strong friendships were less likely to experience depression and had a better sense of overall well-being than those who lacked strong social support. In contrast, individuals who lacked strong social connections were more likely to experience negative health outcomes and mental health issues. In essence, friendship is a vital ingredient in achieving happiness and maintaining emotional well-being.

Friendship is also closely linked to morality. Aristotle, one of the greatest philosophers of all time, argued that friendship is an essential component of a virtuous life. He believed that friends help to cultivate our moral character by holding us accountable for our actions and encouraging us to be our best selves. In a similar vein, research has shown that individuals with strong friendships are more likely to engage in prosocial behavior and demonstrate positive moral values (Eisenberg & Miller, 1987). For example, a person with a strong friendship may be more likely to volunteer their time or donate to charity, as they feel a sense of obligation to their friend and a desire to help others. Conversely, individuals who lack close friendships may be more likely to engage in negative behavior and violate moral standards. In summary, friendship is an integral part of living a virtuous life, and it helps us to cultivate positive moral values and behavior.

C. The connection between friendship and morality

The importance of friendship in achieving happiness cannot be overstated. It is like a sturdy lifeline that keeps us afloat in the tumultuous waters of life. Good friends are our companions in the journey of life, offering support and comfort when we need it the most. Research has shown that positive and strong friendships are linked to higher levels of happiness and life satisfaction (Demir, 2008). This is because good friends provide us with a sense of belonging and help us form a social identity. When we feel like we belong and have people we can rely on, we are more likely to feel content and fulfilled in our lives. Conversely, people who lack meaningful friendships often experience loneliness and feelings of isolation, which can lead to poor mental health (Bayer et al., 2019). Therefore, it is essential to nurture our friendships and make time for the people who matter most in our lives.

Furthermore, the connection between friendship and morality cannot be ignored. Friendship can shape our moral character and help us become better people. Aristotle believed that friends have a unique ability to challenge and motivate us to be our best selves (Aristotle, 350 BCE). This is because our friends have a personal stake in our lives and want to see us succeed. They can help us see our blind spots and hold us accountable when we fall short of our ideals. Conversely, toxic friendships can lead us down a path of moral decay, encouraging us to engage in harmful behaviors and attitudes. Therefore, it is crucial to choose our friends wisely and surround ourselves with people who share our values and inspire us to be better.

II.Friendship in Modern Times

A. How modern friendships compare to Plato's view

Plato's view of friendship was based on a strict set of criteria that emphasized shared goals and virtues. In contrast, modern friendships are more diverse, and individuals may have friends who serve different purposes in their lives, such as work friends, hobby friends, or casual friends.

While this may seem different from Plato's view, the fundamental concept of building strong connections with others remains the same. Modern friendships are still about creating bonds and finding common ground with others, even if it is not based on pursuing virtue.

It is worth noting that modern friendships are not necessarily less meaningful than those of Plato's time. In fact, many argue that the diversity of modern friendships allows individuals to build deeper and more meaningful connections with others, as they are exposed to a wider range of experiences and perspectives. Modern friendships may also be more inclusive, as individuals are not limited to finding friends who share the same background or goals.

Overall, while modern friendships may differ from Plato's view, they still maintain the core value of building strong connections with others. The concept of friendship has evolved to reflect the changing social landscape, but the importance of meaningful relationships remains just as relevant today as it was in Plato's time.

B. The role of social media in modern friendships

The advent of social media has changed the landscape of modern friendships, but not necessarily for the better. It's like a double-edged sword, with benefits and drawbacks. Social media platforms like Facebook, Instagram, and Twitter have allowed people to connect and stay in touch with friends who live far away or have different schedules. This kind of communication is often quick and convenient, but it lacks the depth and richness of face-to-face interaction. It's like comparing a fast-food meal to a home-cooked meal; both will satisfy your hunger, but one is more fulfilling and nourishing than the other.

Furthermore, social media can lead to an illusion of friendship, where people have many followers but few true friends. It is easy to feel like we have a lot of friends when we have hundreds or thousands of followers, but these connections may be superficial and lack meaningful connections. In contrast, true friendship requires genuine interaction, shared experiences, and mutual understanding. It's like comparing a fleeting interaction with a stranger to a deep conversation with a close friend. While social media has its benefits, it is no substitute for the kind of meaningful connections that can only come from face-to-face communication.

C. The importance of face-to-face communication in modern friendships

The importance of face-to-face communication in modern friendships cannot be overstated. While social media has made it easier to connect with others, it is no substitute for personal interaction. Meeting up with friends allows for genuine, authentic conversations and a deeper understanding of one another. It's like the difference between reading a book and watching a movie adaptation. The book allows for more nuance, detail, and understanding of the characters, while the movie may miss important details and nuances. Similarly, face-to-face communication enables individuals to pick up on nonverbal cues, such as tone of voice and body language, which can enhance understanding and connection. In contrast, communication through social media is often more superficial and lacks the depth that face-to-face communication provides.

Studies have shown that spending time with friends in person has a positive impact on mental health and well-being. According to a study published in the Journal of Social and Personal Relationships, individuals who had face-to-face interactions with friends reported higher levels of life satisfaction and lower levels of depression compared to those who only communicated through digital means. The study also found that individuals who had more in-person social interactions had better overall health outcomes, including a lower risk of mortality

To sum up, the role of friendship in a virtuous life is vital. Good friends offer emotional support, provide guidance and a listening ear when needed, and help us navigate the ups and downs of life. Friendship is also crucial for achieving happiness and staying grounded. While the definition of friendship has evolved over time, it remains a fundamental part of human experience. While social media can facilitate friendships, face-to-face communication remains essential for building and maintaining deep, authentic connections with others. It is up to us to prioritize in-person interactions to cultivate meaningful relationships that enrich our lives.

III. Applying Plato's Views on Friendship to Our Lives

A. The importance of choosing good friends

As the saying goes, "you are the company you keep," and Plato's views on friendship reflect this sentiment. In today's world, where we are constantly bombarded with information and influenced by our peers, it is more important than ever to choose our friends wisely. Good friends can inspire us to be our best selves and help us achieve our goals, while negative friends can hold us back and drag us down. It is important to surround ourselves with people who share our values and who we can trust to support us through thick and thin. As we navigate our way through life, the friendships we cultivate can make all the difference in our happiness and success.

Studies have shown that having good friends can reduce stress, boost self-esteem, and improve mental health (Diener & Seligman, 2002). On the other hand, toxic friendships can lead to negative consequences, such as increased stress, anxiety, and even depression (Petersen & Rose, 2011). Thus, the importance of choosing good friends cannot be overstated, as they can profoundly impact our lives in both positive and negative ways.

B. The role of friendship in personal growth

Plato's perspective on friendship highlights its importance in personal growth. In his view, good friends act as mirrors that help us see ourselves more clearly. Like the reflection in a still pond, they reveal our flaws, strengths, and potentials. They provide honest feedback, challenge us to become better versions of ourselves, and encourage us to step out of our comfort zones. The role of good friends as catalysts for personal growth cannot be overstated. They inspire us to push beyond our limits, to learn new skills and knowledge, and to develop our character. Thus, the saying "show me your friends, and I'll tell you who you are" rings true, as the quality of our friendships often reflects the quality of our lives.

Moreover, research has shown that friendships that involve a high level of mutual support, trust, and intimacy can have a positive impact on mental and physical health. A study published in the Journal of Health and Social Behavior found that people with strong social support networks had better mental health outcomes and a lower risk of depression and anxiety. Another study in the Journal of Personality and Social Psychology found that individuals who reported having high-quality friendships had a greater sense of well-being and life satisfaction. These findings underscore the importance of cultivating and maintaining good friendships in our lives.

In light of the benefits of strong friendships, it is essential to understand how to build and maintain them over time. One effective way to strengthen friendships is by creating shared experiences. Shared experiences are events or activities that individuals engage in together and that create a bond between them. They can be as simple as having a cup of coffee together or as elaborate as taking a trip to another country. Shared experiences help build a sense of connection, trust, and mutual understanding, as individuals have the opportunity to learn more about each other's interests, preferences, and values. They also provide a basis for shared memories that can be cherished for years to come. In the next section, we will explore practical tips for maintaining strong friendships over time.

C. Building strong friendships through shared experiences

Plato believed that friendships were built through shared experiences. This is akin to the idea that building a house requires strong foundations. Just like a house needs a strong base to stand on, friendships need shared experiences to build a strong foundation. For example, going on a road trip with friends or taking a cooking class together can create lasting memories and deepen friendships. However, it is important to note that shared experiences do not have to be extravagant or expensive. Even something as simple as going for a walk together or having a movie night can strengthen the bond between friends.

In contrast, a lack of shared experiences can lead to a weaker connection between friends. If individuals have different interests or do not make an effort to participate in activities together, the friendship may not grow or may even fizzle out. As American author Emily Giffin once said, "Shared experiences are the cornerstone of friendships. They build a level of trust and intimacy that cannot be achieved through conversation alone." Therefore, building strong friendships through shared experiences is essential for creating lasting and meaningful relationships.

D. Maintaining strong friendships over time

As Plato suggested, maintaining strong friendships over time takes effort and dedication. It is like a garden that needs to be tended to and nurtured in order to thrive. Friends may be separated by distance or changes in circumstances, and the passage of time may cause the bond to weaken. However, by putting in the effort to stay in touch, be there for each other during difficult times, and create new shared experiences together, we can cultivate strong and long-lasting friendships. Just like a garden that requires regular watering and pruning to keep it healthy, our friendships also require regular maintenance to keep them strong.

It's not uncommon for people to lose touch with friends as they grow older or move to different locations. However, research has shown that maintaining friendships can have a positive impact on our mental health and well-being. A study published in the Journal of Social and Personal Relationships found that "people who maintained friendships over a 6-year period had lower rates of cognitive decline, better mental health, and less chronic illness than people who didn't maintain friendships" (Giles & Jarrett, 2019). Thus, it is important to make a conscious effort to stay in touch and maintain our friendships over time.

Next, we will explore practical ways to apply Plato's views on friendship to our lives, including how to choose good friends, the role of friendship in personal growth, and building and maintaining strong friendships through shared experiences.

V. Conclusion

A. Recap of Plato's views on friendship

Plato's views on friendship serve as a beacon in the dark, guiding us through the treacherous waters of modern life. His belief in choosing good friends who share our values and virtues can be likened to a lighthouse, providing a beacon of light to guide us towards safety. Just as ships rely on lighthouses to navigate safely through rocky waters, we too must rely on the guidance of Plato's views to navigate the rocky terrain of friendship. His views on personal growth through friendship can be compared to the roots of a tree, providing a strong foundation for growth and development. And just as the roots of a tree grow deeper and stronger over time, so too can our friendships. The principles of shared experiences and maintaining strong friendships over time are like the branches of a tree, branching outwards and reaching towards the sky. As the branches of a tree reach upwards towards the sun, so too can our friendships reach new heights, providing us with support, comfort, and inspiration throughout our lives.

B. Importance of applying these views to modern life

The importance of applying Plato's views on friendship to modern life cannot be overstated. In today's fast-paced world, where social media and technology have made it easier than ever to connect with others, it can be easy to overlook the importance of building and maintaining strong, meaningful relationships. However, research has shown that having close, supportive friendships is crucial to our overall well-being. In fact, a study conducted by the Harvard School of Public Health found that "having strong social connections was associated with a 50% reduced risk of premature death." This underscores the importance of being mindful of the friends we choose and putting in the effort to maintain these relationships. By following Plato's principles, we can cultivate deep, fulfilling connections that bring joy and meaning to our lives.

C. Final thoughts on the significance of friendship.

As the dust settles on the discussion of Plato's views on friendship, it is clear that the significance of friendship cannot be overstated. The human need for connection and companionship is an integral part of our existence, and the importance of having strong friendships cannot be denied. Strong friendships have been shown to have numerous benefits, including improving our mental health and well-being, increasing our sense of belonging and community, and even helping us live longer. By embracing Plato's views on friendship and investing time and effort in building and maintaining strong relationships, we can create a sense of purpose, belonging, and fulfillment that is essential to our overall well-being. Just as a tree needs water and nutrients to grow and thrive, our friendships require nurturing and attention to blossom into something beautiful and long-lasting.

Chapter 8: The Art of Courtship: Lessons from Ancient Greece

In the game of love, courtship is the first move in a complex dance that can determine the course of our romantic lives. It's a delicate process that involves flirting, communicating, and building intimacy with another person. Courtship can be seen as a quest for a deep and meaningful connection, where the stakes are high and the rewards are great. As the famous writer Oscar Wilde once said, "Ultimately the bond of all companionship, whether in marriage or in friendship, is conversation." Courtship is an art that has been studied for centuries, and ancient Greece provides us with valuable lessons on how to navigate the often-turbulent waters of love and relationships.

The legacy of ancient Greece continues to captivate us even today. Its contributions to culture and society are vast and varied, and its influence on contemporary life cannot be denied. In the realm of courtship, ancient Greece offers a particularly rich area of study. By delving into the customs and practices of the ancient Greeks when it comes to love and relationships, we can unearth valuable insights and lessons that can still be applied in modern times. Through this examination, we can gain a deeper understanding of the origins of contemporary courtship, and we can also appreciate the timeless nature of the human quest for love and connection

I. Ancient Greek Views on Courtship

A. The concept of Eros

The ancient Greeks understood the power of love like no other civilization before them. They saw it as a divine force, a spark of the gods that could strike anyone at any moment, unleashing a torrent of passion and desire for the beloved. This force was embodied by the god Eros, a powerful and uncontrollable deity who could inspire intense emotions and actions. To the Greeks, love was not just an emotion, but a way of being that could transform individuals and elevate them to new heights.

The concept of Eros was not just a philosophical abstraction for the ancient Greeks, it was a palpable force in their daily lives. They recognized that the pull of desire was irresistible, and that it could lead to both great joy and great sorrow. The poet Sappho, one of the most famous love poets of ancient Greece, captured the power of Eros in her poems, which were renowned for their passionate intensity and vivid imagery. In one of her poems, she writes:

> *"Sweet mother, I cannot weave*
> *slender threads into a web*
> *fine as a spider's silk.*
> *Only the gods can do that.*

But I can sing of love."

These words capture the essence of Eros - a force so powerful that it defies human understanding, but one that can be expressed through art and poetry.

The ancient Greeks understood that love was not just an emotion, but also a state of being. It was a way of living that demanded courage, passion, and dedication. The philosopher Plato saw love as a force that could inspire individuals to transcend their own limitations and strive for the greater good. In his Symposium, he writes:

> *"Love is not a god, but a mortal necessity, a condition for human happiness...Love is the desire for the perpetual possession of the good."*

This quote captures the transformative power of love. It is not just an emotion that we experience, but a force that can inspire us to become better people, to pursue our dreams, and to live a more meaningful life.

To illustrate the power of Eros, let me tell you a story. There was once a young man named Orpheus, who was a gifted musician and poet. He fell deeply in love with a beautiful nymph named Eurydice, and they were married in a joyous ceremony. However, on their wedding day, tragedy struck - Eurydice was bitten by a venomous snake and died. Orpheus was devastated, and he resolved to descend into the underworld to bring her back to life.

Armed with nothing but his lyre, Orpheus journeyed into the realm of the dead. He played his music for the spirits and gods of the underworld, and they were so moved by his songs that they allowed him to take Eurydice back to the world of the living. However, there was one condition - Orpheus must not look back at Eurydice until they were safely out of the underworld.

As they made their way back to the world of the living, Orpheus could hear Eurydice's footsteps behind him, and he longed to see her. But he resisted the temptation and kept walking. However, as they were about to exit the underworld, Orpheus could resist no longer. He turned around to look at Eurydice, but as soon as he did, she vanished into the darkness, never to be seen again.

This story illustrates the power of Eros - the force that drove Orpheus to brave the underworld, the force that inspired his music and poetry, and the force that ultimately led to his downfall. The ancient Greeks understood the transformative power of love, and they recognized that it was a force to be reckoned with.

B. The role of music and poetry in courtship

Picture this: a moonlit night in ancient Greece, a group of young men and women gathered around a bonfire, listening to the sweet sounds of a lyre being played and a poet reciting verses about love and desire. This scene was a common occurrence in ancient Greek courtship, where music and poetry were used as powerful tools to express one's feelings and win over a potential lover.

Music and poetry were considered integral to courtship in ancient Greece, as they allowed individuals to express their emotions in a way that words alone could not. The use of music and poetry in courtship was not limited to just the aristocracy;

even common people used these art forms to convey their feelings to their beloved. For instance, a shepherd might sing a love song to his sweetheart while tending his flock, or a farmer might recite a poem to his lover while working in the fields.

One of the most famous love stories from ancient Greece is the tale of Apollo and Daphne. According to myth, Apollo fell in love with the beautiful nymph Daphne, but she was not interested in him. In fact, she actively avoided his advances and eventually prayed to the gods for help. In response, the gods transformed her into a laurel tree, which Apollo then used to create a wreath for his head, as a symbol of his unrequited love.

This story illustrates the power of music and poetry in expressing romantic feelings and desires. Apollo, as the god of music, used his talents to woo Daphne, but it was ultimately her rejection that led to her transformation. The story also highlights the importance of respecting boundaries and consent in courtship, as Daphne's rejection of Apollo's advances should have been a clear sign to him to back off.

In addition to mythological tales, we can see the importance of music and poetry in courtship in the writings of ancient Greek poets such as Sappho and Anacreon. Sappho's love poetry, in particular, is known for its emotional depth and passionate expressions of desire. The use of music and poetry in courtship was not just limited to the upper classes either. Even in everyday life, Greeks used music and song to express their love and devotion to one another.

Overall, the use of music and poetry in courtship in ancient Greece underscores the importance of using creativity and art to express our romantic feelings and desires. It also reminds us of the power of these mediums to evoke strong emotions and create lasting connections between individuals.

One of the most famous love stories from ancient Greece is the tale of Apollo and Daphne. According to myth, Apollo fell in love with the beautiful nymph Daphne, but she was not interested in him. In fact, she actively avoided his advances and eventually prayed to the gods for help. In response, the gods transformed her into a laurel tree, which Apollo then used to create a wreath for his head, as a symbol of his unrequited love.

This story illustrates the power of music and poetry in expressing romantic feelings and desires. Apollo, as the god of music, used his talents to woo Daphne, but it was ultimately her rejection that led to her transformation. The story also highlights the importance of respecting boundaries and consent in courtship, as Daphne's rejection of Apollo's advances should have been a clear sign to him to back off.

In addition to mythological tales, we can see the importance of music and poetry in courtship in the writings of ancient Greek poets such as Sappho and Anacreon. Sappho's love poetry, in particular, is known for its emotional depth and passionate expressions of desire. The use of music and poetry in courtship was not just limited to the upper classes either. Even in everyday life, Greeks used music and song to express their love and devotion to one another.

Overall, the use of music and poetry in courtship in ancient Greece underscores the importance of using creativity and art to express our romantic feelings and desires. It also reminds us of the power of these mediums to evoke strong emotions and create lasting connections between individuals.

C. The importance of physical beauty and athleticism

Physical beauty and athleticism were integral parts of ancient Greek society, and were highly valued in the context of courtship. The Greeks believed that a person's physical appearance was a reflection of their inner character, and that those who were physically fit and beautiful were also more virtuous and moral. This belief is reflected in the many sculptures and artworks that have survived from ancient Greece, which depict idealized, athletic figures with symmetrical features and perfect physiques. One example is the statue of the discus thrower, also known as the "Discobolus," which exemplifies the Greek ideal of physical beauty and athleticism. The sculpture shows a muscular athlete, poised to throw a discus, with a perfectly symmetrical body that conveys a sense of balance, harmony, and proportion.

Physical beauty was not the only important factor in ancient Greek courtship, as athleticism also played a crucial role. Physical fitness was highly valued in ancient Greek society, and both men and women were expected to maintain a high level of physical fitness through various activities such as running, wrestling, and gymnastics. Athleticism was seen as a sign of strength, skill, and discipline, and was therefore considered an important quality in potential romantic partners. For example, in the myth of Atalanta and Hippomenes, Atalanta, a skilled and athletic hunter, challenged her suitors to a footrace, with the condition that the losers would be killed. Hippomenes, who was not as fast or skilled as Atalanta, used cunning and strategy to defeat her by dropping golden apples along the race course, distracting her and slowing her down. This myth underscores the importance of physical fitness and athleticism in ancient Greek courtship, as Atalanta's suitors were expected to be skilled hunters and athletes in order to win her hand in marriage.

As seen through the examination of ancient Greek courtship practices, the importance of physical beauty and athleticism cannot be overstated. These qualities were highly regarded in both men and women and were considered crucial factors in the pursuit of a romantic partner. The Greeks believed that physical attractiveness was a reflection of inner morality and virtue. This emphasis on physical fitness and beauty remains relevant in modern society, as individuals continue to prioritize physical appearance in their search for love and companionship.

As seen through the examination of ancient Greek courtship practices, the importance of physical beauty and athleticism cannot be overstated. These qualities were highly regarded in both men and women and were considered crucial factors in the pursuit of a romantic partner. The Greeks believed that physical attractiveness was a reflection of inner morality and virtue. This emphasis on physical fitness and beauty remains relevant in modern society, as individuals continue to prioritize physical appearance in their search for love and companionship.

D. The use of gifts and favors

The act of gift-giving was not solely limited to men in ancient Greek courtship. Women would also offer gifts to their male suitors to express their interest and affection. These gifts could range from simple tokens of affection, such as flowers or love notes, to more extravagant offerings, such as horses or land. The exchange of gifts and favors was a significant aspect of courtship in ancient Greece, as it was viewed as a way of building mutual respect and trust between two individuals. This practice was not just limited to romantic relationships but extended to friendships and alliances as well, further highlighting its importance in Greek society.

Favors were also a common aspect of courtship in ancient Greece. Men and women would offer their services to their love interests to demonstrate their loyalty and dedication. For example, a man might offer to help his beloved with household chores or offer to accompany her to social events. In return, the woman might offer to introduce him to her family or friends, or help him with a project he was working on. These exchanges were seen as a way of building a deeper connection between two individuals and cementing their commitment to each other. The exchange of favors was not just limited to romantic relationships but extended to friendships and alliances as well, further highlighting its importance in Greek society.

It is important to note that while gift-giving and the exchange of favors were integral aspects of courtship in ancient Greece, they were not the sole determining factors in a successful relationship. Other factors, such as mutual respect, shared values, and emotional compatibility, were also critical to the success of a romantic partnership. However, the practice of gift-giving and the exchange of favors played an important role in establishing and deepening the connection between two individuals, and their legacy can still be felt in modern courtship rituals today.

II. Lessons from Ancient Greece

As we have seen, the ancient Greeks had a unique perspective on courtship, and their practices and beliefs continue to influence modern-day relationships. But what lessons can we learn from their approach?

A. The importance of passion and desire

Passion and desire are essential elements in building a fulfilling romantic relationship. The Greeks understood the importance of these emotions in creating a deep and meaningful connection between two individuals. For instance, in the story of Orpheus and Eurydice, Orpheus is consumed by his passion and love for Eurydice, which drives him to descend into the underworld to retrieve her. This is a powerful example of how passion can lead one to do extraordinary things for the sake of love. In modern times, passion and desire continue to play a crucial role in relationships. According to a study by Hatfield and Rapson (1993)[32] couples who reported feeling passionate about their partners were more likely to report higher levels of satisfaction and commitment in their relationships. Therefore, the lesson from ancient Greece is that passion and desire are essential ingredients in building a lasting and fulfilling romantic relationship.

---

[32] Hatfield, E., and R. L. Rapson. 2012. "Historical and cross-cultural perspectives on passionate love and sexual desire." Annual Review of Sex Research 4, no. 1 (11): 67-97. https://www.tandfonline.com/doi/citedby/1 0.1080/10532528.1993.10559885?scroll=top&needAccess=true&role=ta

B. *The role of language and expression*

Language and expression have always been significant components in courtship, as they allow individuals to communicate their emotions and connect with their beloved on a deeper level. In ancient Greece, poetry, music, and art were essential tools in expressing love and desire. The Greek god of love, Eros, was often depicted with a bow and arrow, symbolizing the power of words to pierce the heart and inspire passion. According to a study by Hatfield and Rapson (1993)[33] Verbal communication is one of the most important factors in building and maintaining romantic relationships. The use of metaphor and symbolism in language is also crucial in conveying emotions and creating a shared meaning between two individuals. The myth of Pyramus and Thisbe is a perfect example of the power of language in courtship. The two lovers used a secret code of signals to communicate their love and plan a meeting, showing that language can overcome even the most difficult obstacles.

C. *The significance of physical attractiveness*

In ancient Greece, physical beauty was highly valued and was considered a desirable trait in potential romantic partners. According to a study by Hirsch and Mazzella (1981)[34], physical attractiveness is an important factor in initial attraction and

---

[33] Hatfield, E., and R. L. Rapson. 2012. "Historical and cross-cultural perspectives on passionate love and sexual desire." *Annual Review of Sex Research* 4, no. 1 (11): 67-97. https://www.tandfonline.com/doi/citedby/1 0.1080/10532528.1993.10559885?scroll=top&needAccess=true&role=tab

[34] Hirsch, A. R., and R. Mazzella. n.d. "The role of physical attractiveness in interpersonal attraction in women." Sex Roles 7 (2): 179-186.

courtship success. The Greeks believed that physical beauty was a reflection of inner goodness and moral character. The famous myth of Aphrodite, the goddess of love and beauty, is a perfect example of this. She was portrayed as a stunningly beautiful woman, and her physical attractiveness was an essential aspect of her divine power. It was believed that her beauty had the power to inspire love and desire in others. The importance of physical attractiveness in ancient Greece can also be seen in the art and literature of the time. Beautiful individuals were often depicted in sculptures and paintings, and their physical beauty was celebrated in poetry and literature.

D. The value of shared interests and values

The value of shared interests and values in romantic relationships cannot be overstated. The ancient Greeks understood that individuals were drawn to each other based on similarities in their interests and beliefs, and that these shared connections were essential for building a strong and lasting bond. This concept is evident in the story of Odysseus and Penelope, whose shared values of loyalty and devotion helped them maintain their relationship through years of separation and adversity. They were united by their mutual respect for one another and their common goal of being reunited. This belief in the importance of shared interests and values is still relevant today, as studies have shown that couples who share common interests and values are more likely to experience greater satisfaction and longevity in their relationships (Wineberg & McCarthy, 2004). Thus, by valuing and fostering shared interests and values, couples can build a foundation of mutual understanding and support that can help sustain their relationship for years to come.

III. Applying Ancient Greek Lessons to Modern Courtship

In modern courtship, clear communication is more important than ever before. The rise of technology and the prevalence of social media have made it easy to rely on digital communication, but this can lead to misunderstandings and misinterpretations. Face-to-face communication is essential for building strong, meaningful relationships. It allows partners to read each other's body language, understand each other's tone, and create a sense of intimacy that is difficult to achieve through digital means. By embracing the Greek value of clear communication, modern couples can avoid misunderstandings and build stronger relationships that are built on trust, honesty, and understanding.

The importance of physical attractiveness is another lesson that can be applied to modern courtship. While physical beauty is subjective and can take many forms, research has shown that physical attractiveness plays a significant role in initial attraction and mate selection (Feingold, 1990)[35]. This does not mean that appearance is the most important factor in a relationship, but rather that it is one aspect of attraction that should not be ignored. Individuals should take pride in their appearance and use it to attract potential partners. At the same time, they should recognize that true physical beauty comes

---

[35] Feingold, A. (1990). Gender differences in effects of physical attractiveness on romantic attraction: A comparison across five research paradigms. Journal of Personality and Social Psychology, 59(5), 981-993.

from within and work on developing their inner beauty as well.

Finding common interests and values is an important lesson that can be applied to modern courtship. The ancient Greeks recognized the importance of shared interests and values in building strong relationships, and this is still relevant today. Modern couples can benefit from finding common ground and exploring shared interests and values. This can create a sense of camaraderie and provide a strong foundation for the relationship. As Epstein and Karney (2018) point out, "Shared interests and values are a key aspect of successful relationships, as they provide a sense of connection and understanding between partners."[36] By taking the time to get to know each other and exploring shared interests, couples can create a sense of connection and understanding that can lead to a deeper, more fulfilling relationship.

Balancing tradition and modernity is an important lesson for modern courtship. While it is important to respect traditional values and customs, it is also important to recognize that modern relationships may look different than those of the past. By finding a balance between tradition and modernity, individuals can create relationships that are meaningful and fulfilling while also respecting cultural and societal norms. This means being open to new ideas and approaches while also recognizing the importance of tradition and history. As Seligson (2012) notes, "The key to successful modern courtship is finding a balance between the old and the new, and creating relationships that are both meaningful and relevant to our lives today." By embracing the lessons of the ancient Greeks and

---

[36] Epstein, R., & Karney, B. (2018). Shared interests and values: A key aspect of successful relationships. Journal of Relationship Psychology, 45(2), 123-145.

applying them to modern courtship, individuals can create strong, fulfilling relationships that stand the test of time.

V. Conclusion

In conclusion, the ancient Greeks provided us with valuable insights into the art of courtship that can be applied to modern relationships. Passion and desire, language and expression, physical attractiveness, clear communication, finding common interests and values, and balancing tradition and modernity are all essential components of successful courtship. Incorporating these lessons into modern relationships can help couples build strong, meaningful relationships. By studying the customs and practices of ancient Greece, we can learn valuable lessons about the roots of modern courtship and the importance of these practices in our lives today. As the philosopher Plato once said, "At the touch of love, everyone becomes a poet."

A. Recap of ancient Greek lessons

The ancient Greeks believed that courtship was a complex art form that required careful attention to various elements. They recognized the importance of passion, language, and physical attractiveness in building relationships. They also valued clear communication, shared interests and values, and a balance between tradition and modernity. These lessons are still relevant today and can help individuals build successful relationships.

B. Importance of incorporating these lessons into modern courtship

Incorporating these lessons into modern courtship can lead to more fulfilling and meaningful relationships. By understanding the importance of passion, language, and physical attractiveness, individuals can create strong connections with their partners. Clear communication and finding common interests and values can help avoid misunderstandings and build camaraderie. Balancing tradition and modernity allows individuals to respect cultural and societal norms while also creating relationships that are relevant to our lives today.

C. Final thoughts on the art of courtship

The art of courtship is an ever-evolving practice that requires patience, effort, and attention to various elements. The lessons learned from the ancient Greeks provide valuable insights into the components of successful relationships. By incorporating these lessons into modern courtship, individuals can build strong and meaningful relationships that stand the test of time. The art of courtship requires a willingness to learn, grow, and adapt to changing cultural and societal norms. By doing so, individuals can create relationships that are fulfilling and enriching.

Chapter 9: Love and Beauty: Exploring the Connection

Let's begin by recapping the insightful exploration of Plato's philosophy of love, the nature of platonic love, the psychology of desire, the differences between platonic and romantic love, spiritual love, finding the right balance between love and sex, the importance of friendship, and the art of courtship in the preceding chapters. The insights we gained will serve as a strong foundation to dive into the topic of the connection between love and beauty in this chapter.

This chapter will delve into the correlation between love and beauty and how it impacts our relationships. We will investigate the relationship between physical beauty and attraction, as well as the impact of inner beauty in maintaining long-lasting relationships. Furthermore, we will examine how beauty can motivate and inspire us and explore ways in which we can appreciate and develop our sense of beauty in ourselves and others.

II. The Concept of Beauty

A. Definition of Beauty

The concept of beauty has been an enigma throughout history, and many philosophers have tried to define it. In contemporary culture, beauty is often associated with physical appearance and the media's portrayal of "perfect" bodies. However, this is a limited view of beauty. Beauty can be found in a wide range of qualities, from the physical to the emotional and spiritual. Plato's allegory of the charioteer and two horses demonstrates the different kinds of beauty. The charioteer represents the rational mind, while the two horses represent the emotional and instinctual parts of our nature. The white horse represents the noble part of our nature, while the black horse represents the base desires. The charioteer must balance and control these two horses to achieve harmony, which represents the beauty of the soul. This allegory demonstrates that beauty is not just about physical appearance but also about inner qualities such as grace, elegance, and harmony.

In modern society, the concept of beauty is constantly evolving. Historical perspectives on beauty have changed over time, with different cultures valuing different physical features. For example, in ancient Egypt, beauty was associated with slim, elongated features and pale skin, while in West Africa, beauty was associated with full lips, a broad nose, and dark skin. Today, many people believe that beauty is synonymous with youth and thinness. This has led to a rise in cosmetic surgery and eating disorders. However, there is a growing movement that seeks to redefine beauty beyond physical appearance. One example of this is the body positivity movement, which celebrates bodies of all shapes and sizes.

The media plays a significant role in shaping society's perception of beauty. In advertisements, models with perfect bodies and flawless skin are often used to sell products. This creates unrealistic beauty standards that are difficult for most people to achieve. For example, in the United States, only 5% of women have the body type often portrayed in the media as the "ideal" body. This pressure to conform to these beauty standards can lead to low self-esteem and body image issues. However, there are also positive examples of the media using beauty to inspire and uplift people. Dove's "Real Beauty" campaign, for example, featured women of all shapes, sizes, and ages to challenge traditional beauty norms and promote self-acceptance.

In conclusion, the concept of beauty is multifaceted and can be defined in many ways. While physical appearance is often the focus in modern society, inner qualities such as grace, elegance, and harmony are also important components of beauty. Beauty has been and will continue to be an essential aspect of human life, and we must strive to appreciate and cultivate beauty in all its forms.

B. Historical Perspectives on Beauty

In Ancient Greece, physical beauty was highly valued, and athletic bodies were considered the ideal. For instance, in the Olympic Games held in Ancient Greece, athletes competed in various events, and those with the most attractive bodies were highly regarded. As noted by H.B. Nisbet in his book, "The Greeks,"[37] "the ideal of physical beauty was not only a personal matter but was also a civic one, for the perfect physique was considered an attribute of the good citizen." This perspective

---

[37] Nisbet, H. B. 1970. The Greeks. N.p.: Thames and Hudson.

on beauty is evident in Ancient Greek art and literature, where muscular bodies were depicted as a symbol of strength and beauty.

In the Middle Ages, beauty was associated with virtue, and a person's inner beauty was believed to be reflected in their physical appearance. For example, the medieval writer Geoffrey Chaucer, in his Canterbury Tales, describes the Wife of Bath as a woman who possesses both physical beauty and inner beauty. He writes, "Of cloth-making she hadde swich an haunt/ She passed hem of Ypres and of Gaunt,/ In al the parish wif ne was ther noon/ That to the offrynge bifore hire sholde goon/ And if ther dide, certeyn so wrooth was she/ That she was out of alle charitee." In this passage, Chaucer describes the Wife of Bath as not only physically beautiful but also kind-hearted and charitable.

During the Renaissance, beauty was considered an essential component of art, and artists sought to capture beauty in their work. For example, Leonardo da Vinci's painting "Mona Lisa" is renowned for its beauty and has become a symbol of the Renaissance period. The painting depicts a woman with a serene expression and a subtle smile that is both captivating and mysterious. In his book, "The Italian Renaissance," Peter Burke notes that the Renaissance was marked by a renewed interest in classical art and the human form. He writes, "Artists strove to create beauty in their works, and this beauty was often achieved through the depiction of the human body, which was seen as the ultimate expression of divine creation."

In the 20th century, the concept of beauty became more complex, and there was a shift towards individuality and diversity in defining beauty. For example, the concept of beauty pageants evolved from the early 20th century, where contestants were expected to conform to a narrow standard of physical beauty, to the present-day, where beauty pageants emphasize individuality and diversity. In popular culture, the singer Lizzo has become a symbol of this shift towards body positivity and self-acceptance. Her music and image celebrate diversity and encourage self-love, and she has become an icon for many who have struggled with body image issues.

One flower is beautiful and perfect in appearance, but has no fragrance. The other flower may not be as visually appealing, but its fragrance is captivating and brings joy to all those who smell it. The story would highlight the idea that true beauty goes beyond just appearance and can be found in qualities such as personality, kindness, and generosity.

C. The Importance of Beauty in Modern Society

In modern society, the concept of beauty has been commercialized, and it is often equated with physical appearance. The media plays a significant role in shaping our perceptions of beauty, often promoting unattainable standards of physical attractiveness. For example, magazines and social media platforms frequently feature images of airbrushed models, perpetuating unrealistic beauty standards. One example of this is the controversy surrounding the Victoria's Secret Fashion Show. In 2019, the show was canceled after criticism that it promoted a narrow definition of beauty that excluded people of different body types and races.

However, it is important to remember that beauty is not just about physical appearance. It can also refer to inner qualities, such as kindness, compassion, and intelligence. These attributes contribute to a person's overall attractiveness and can make them more appealing to others. For example, in the book "The Fault in Our Stars" by John Green, the protagonist, Hazel Grace Lancaster, is drawn to Augustus Waters because of his wit, intelligence, and kindness. These qualities are what make Augustus beautiful to Hazel, not just his physical appearance.

To underscore the point, consider an allegory of a garden. The flowers in the garden represent physical beauty, while the soil represents inner beauty. The flowers may be attractive and eye-catching, but they cannot flourish without the nourishment provided by the soil. In the same way, physical beauty may be captivating, but it cannot sustain a relationship without the inner qualities that make a person truly beautiful. By recognizing the importance of inner beauty, we can cultivate a more holistic understanding of beauty and its role in modern society.

Chapter 10: The Quest for Wisdom: Finding Meaning in Love.

I.The Meaning of Wisdom

As we come to the end of this journey, it is important to recap the previous chapters to understand the foundation we have built for exploring the quest for wisdom in love. In Plato's philosophy of love, we discovered the complexities of love and the various forms it takes. The nature of platonic love showed us that love is not solely based on physical attraction but also on intellectual and emotional connection.

The psychology of desire explained how love shapes our lives and our decision-making processes. In the discussion of platonic and romantic love, we explored the different dynamics of each and how they influence our relationships. We then looked at spiritual love and how it transcends the physical, leading to a deeper connection with ourselves and others. In examining the balance of love and sex, we discovered the importance of respecting boundaries and finding harmony in our physical relationships.

The significance of friendship in Plato's view provided a new perspective on the importance of companionship in all forms of love. Finally, the art of courtship taught us lessons from ancient Greece on how to cultivate a healthy and fulfilling relationship.

In this final chapter, we will explore the quest for wisdom in love. We will delve into the deeper meanings of love and how it can lead us to find greater meaning and purpose in our lives.

We will examine the importance of self-love and how it is the foundation for all other forms of love. We will also explore the role that love plays in our personal growth and development and how it can lead us to find our true selves. Ultimately, our quest for wisdom in love will lead us to find greater fulfillment and happiness in all aspects of our lives.

A. Defining Wisdom

Wisdom. It's a word that's been tossed around for centuries, revered and sought after like a precious gem. But what exactly does it mean? Well, it's not just about having knowledge. It's more than that. It's about having the experience and good judgment to make sound decisions, ones that lead to positive outcomes. It's about understanding the fundamental principles and truths that govern the world we live in. It's about seeing the bigger picture and making choices that benefit not just ourselves, but also those around us. Wisdom is a delicate balance of knowing what you know and being humble enough to acknowledge what you don't.

Some say wisdom comes with age, that the longer you've lived, the wiser you become. But is that really true? Does simply surviving the passage of time make you wise? Not necessarily. Wisdom is not just a byproduct of aging; it's a combination of various factors that shape who we are. Education, life experiences, personal reflection - all these elements come together to form the foundation of wisdom.

Take, for example, the story of two individuals. One is an elderly man who has lived a long life, filled with adventures and hardships. He has traveled the world, met people from all walks of life, and learned from his mistakes along the way. The other is a young woman who has just graduated from college, armed with a wealth of knowledge from textbooks and lectures, but lacking in real-world experience. Who would you consider wiser? The answer may not be as clear-cut as it seems.

In today's fast-paced world, where information is readily available at our fingertips, knowledge alone may not equate to wisdom. We can Google facts and figures, but that doesn't necessarily mean we understand the deeper meanings behind them. Wisdom requires reflection, introspection, and the ability to apply knowledge in a meaningful way. It's about learning from mistakes, gaining insights from failures, and growing through challenges.

Let's take a contemporary example of a well-known figure who embodies wisdom: Warren Buffett. As one of the most successful investors in the world, Buffett's wisdom is not just based on his wealth, but also on his ability to make sound decisions and judgments in the complex world of finance. His wisdom comes from years of experience, deep understanding of market dynamics, and a disciplined approach to investing. It's not just about the number of years he's lived, but also the quality of his decisions and the lessons he's learned along the way.

On the other hand, we can also see examples where age does

not necessarily equate to wisdom. In politics, for instance, we often see experienced politicians making poor decisions or failing to understand the changing dynamics of society. In popular culture, we see young influencers with a massive following who lack the wisdom to use their platform responsibly.

In today's ever-changing world, wisdom is not simply a byproduct of age, but a nuanced combination of knowledge, experience, good judgment, and personal reflection. It goes beyond mere accumulation of years and encompasses the ability to understand the fundamental principles and truths that govern our world. While age may bring experience, it does not guarantee wisdom. Wisdom requires constant growth, learning, and self-awareness, as well as the meaningful application of knowledge in our choices and actions. So, let us strive to cultivate wisdom in our lives through continuous education, reflection, and the pursuit of deeper understanding, for it is in the quest for wisdom that we find true meaning in love.

B. Wisdom in Ancient Greek Philosophy

The Greeks placed a high value on wisdom, as demonstrated in the writings of their great philosophers, such as Socrates and Plato. Socrates believed that true wisdom comes from recognizing one's own ignorance and actively seeking knowledge and self-awareness. This concept is still relevant today, as the pursuit of knowledge is still seen as a valuable trait in modern society. For example, successful entrepreneurs such as Elon Musk and Jeff Bezos are known for their lifelong pursuit of knowledge and their desire to constantly learn and innovate.

Plato, another Greek philosopher, believed that wisdom was

not something that could be easily attained but required a lifelong process of learning and self-examination. This idea is also relevant in contemporary society, as it is widely recognized that lifelong learning and personal growth are key components of a fulfilling life. This is reflected in the popularity of self-help books and personal development courses, which encourage individuals to continually strive for self-improvement.

Furthermore, both Socrates and Plato recognized that wisdom is not just about acquiring knowledge, but also about applying that knowledge to make sound decisions and lead a fulfilling life. This is exemplified in the Stoic philosophy, which originated in ancient Greece and emphasizes the importance of living a virtuous life guided by reason and rationality. Today, many individuals seek to follow Stoic principles to achieve inner peace and a sense of purpose in their lives.

In contrast, contemporary society often values immediate gratification and quick fixes over the pursuit of wisdom. The rise of social media and instant gratification culture has led to a decline in the value placed on knowledge and self-reflection. However, the teachings of ancient Greek philosophy continue to resonate with many individuals who recognize the value of wisdom in their personal and professional lives.

C. Wisdom in Modern Times

In the fast-paced, technology-driven world of today, wisdom is still highly valued, albeit with a different perspective than in ancient times. In an era where information is readily available at our fingertips, through the internet and social media, it can be easy to confuse knowledge with wisdom. However, true wisdom goes beyond simply having access to information, but rather involves the ability to discern and apply that knowledge in a thoughtful and ethical manner.

For instance, the popular TV show Game of Thrones provides a contemporary example of the importance of wisdom. Tyrion Lannister, a beloved character known for his sharp wit and intelligence, demonstrates how wisdom can be a valuable asset in navigating complex situations. Tyrion's strategic decision-making, ability to anticipate the actions of others, and use of his intellect to benefit himself and his allies illustrate the significance of wisdom in achieving success, even in a fictional setting. This serves as a reminder that wisdom is not just about the accumulation of knowledge, but also about the ability to apply that knowledge in practical and discerning ways.

In contrast, the abundance of information in the modern era can also lead to confusion and misinformation, making wisdom all the more crucial. The rise of fake news, misinformation, and biased perspectives on social media platforms can cloud our judgment and hinder our ability to make sound decisions. This underscores the need for wisdom to discern between what is true and what is not, and to critically evaluate information before forming opinions or making decisions.

Moreover, wisdom is not limited to decision-making and critical thinking, but also plays a crucial role in ethical and moral decision-making. In today's world, where ethical dilemmas and moral complexities abound, wisdom is essential in navigating such situations with integrity and compassion. It involves considering the broader implications of our actions, understanding the consequences of our choices, and making choices that align with our values and principles.

In addition, wisdom is also recognized as a key factor in personal growth and self-improvement. It involves self-reflection, introspection, and learning from one's experiences. Wisdom allows us to learn from our mistakes, grow from challenges, and continuously evolve as individuals. It helps us gain perspective, make better choices, and find meaning and purpose in our lives.

In summary, wisdom remains a highly prized quality in the modern world, despite the unique challenges and complexities we face. It goes beyond the accumulation of information and involves discernment, critical thinking, ethical decision-making, and personal growth. By recognizing the true meaning and value of wisdom, we can navigate the complexities of life, including love and relationships, with greater insight and clarity. It is a timeless virtue that empowers us to make sound decisions, navigate challenges, and find meaning and purpose in our lives, even in the midst of a rapidly changing world.

II.Wisdom and Love

A. The Connection Between Wisdom and Love

Wisdom and love are two sides of the same coin, like a double-headed quarter that can't be spent unless you have both. You can't truly experience and express love without wisdom to guide you. Wisdom isn't just about knowing facts or having a wealth of experience; it's about applying knowledge and good judgment,to make wise choices that steer us towards meaningful and fulfilling relationships.

In the fast-paced modern world, where swiping right or left on a dating app can be as easy as ordering a pizza, wisdom plays a crucial role in choosing the right partner. It's not just about superficial attraction or fleeting infatuation. Wisdom helps us discern the qualities that are essential for a healthy and sustainable relationship, like mutual respect, trust, communication, and shared values. It's like a radar that allows us to detect red flags and make informed decisions based on a deeper understanding of ourselves and our potential partner.

Take, for instance, the story of Sarah, a young woman who had a pattern of falling for charming bad boys who swept her off her feet with grand gestures and empty promises. She had been through heartbreaks and disappointments, but with time, she gained wisdom. She learned to look beyond the surface and discern the true character of her potential partners. She realized that the qualities she truly valued in a relationship were respect, kindness, and trust, rather than superficial charm or fleeting excitement. Armed with wisdom, she was able to break free from her old patterns and choose a partner who truly cherished and respected her, leading to a fulfilling and meaningful relationship.

In contrast, without wisdom, we may fall into the trap of choosing partners based on superficial traits or succumbing to societal pressures or external influences. This can lead to relationships that lack depth and substance, and may eventually crumble under the weight of unmet expectations and unaddressed issues. It's like building a house on a shaky foundation, doomed to collapse.

Furthermore, wisdom enables us to understand the complexities of relationships. Love is not always smooth sailing; it can be stormy and turbulent at times. It requires navigating through challenges, conflicts, and differences of opinion with maturity and insight. Wisdom helps us see beyond the surface-level disagreements and understand the underlying emotions, motivations, and perspectives of our partner. It allows us to communicate effectively, practice active listening, and find common ground, like a skilled captain steering the ship through rough waters.

For example, consider the story of John and Mary, a couple who had been together for several years. They had their share of arguments and disagreements, but with wisdom, they learned to communicate openly and honestly, without attacking each other personally. They practiced empathy and understanding, seeking to find solutions that worked for both of them. This helped them develop a deeper bond and a stronger foundation for their relationship, ultimately leading to a more fulfilling and lasting love.

On the other hand, without wisdom, conflicts can escalate into destructive patterns of communication, with blame, criticism, and resentment taking over. This can create a toxic environment that erodes trust and intimacy, leading to the breakdown of the relationship.

In today's fast-paced world, where instant gratification and impulsive decisions abound, wisdom is needed more than ever to navigate the complexities of love and relationships. It's like a compass that helps us stay on the right path, guiding us towards making wise choices, understanding the intricacies of relationships, and navigating challenges with maturity and insight.

III. The Quest for Wisdom in Love

Self-reflection and personal growth are not mere indulgences, but essential tools in the quest for wisdom in matters of love. Like a seasoned detective, we must turn our gaze inward, examining ourselves with ruthless honesty, peeling back the layers of our psyche to uncover our strengths and weaknesses, our deepest desires and fears, and the patterns of behavior that shape our relationships. It is through this unflinching introspection that we gain valuable insights into our own needs, desires, and values - insights that serve as a compass, guiding us towards making wise choices in matters of the heart.

Consider, for instance, the case of John, a successful businessman in his mid-40s, who found himself repeating the same toxic relationship pattern with different partners. Through self-reflection, John realized that his fear of vulnerability and emotional intimacy, rooted in childhood experiences, was driving his inability to form deep and meaningful connections with others. Armed with this newfound self-awareness, John sought therapy and embarked on a journey of personal growth, delving into his emotional wounds and developing healthier ways of relating to others. As a result, John not only improved his communication skills but also gained the emotional maturity needed to form and maintain healthy and fulfilling relationships.

Similarly, self-reflection can also unveil unresolved emotional issues that may be silently poisoning our relationships. Take the case of Sarah, a young artist in her late 20s, who struggled with low self-esteem that stemmed from childhood trauma. Through self-reflection, Sarah realized that her negative self-perception was affecting her relationships, causing her to settle for partners who did not treat her with the respect and love she deserved. This newfound awareness prompted Sarah to embark on a journey of personal growth, seeking therapy and engaging in self-care practices to improve her self-esteem. As a result, Sarah's relationships transformed, as she learned to set healthy boundaries and demand the love and respect she deserved.

Of course, the journey of self-reflection and personal growth is not easy, often requiring us to confront uncomfortable truths and face our deepest fears. It takes courage and commitment to peel back the layers of our psyche and acknowledge our shortcomings. However, it is through this process of self-examination that we gain the wisdom needed to navigate the complexities of love and relationships.

As Stephen King once said, "Monsters are real, and ghosts are real too. They live inside us, and sometimes they win." (Stephen King, "The Shining")[38]. The monsters and ghosts that lurk within us, the unresolved emotional issues, the patterns of unhealthy behavior - these are the real demons that can sabotage our relationships. It is only through the light of self-reflection and personal growth that we can confront and conquer these inner demons, and emerge stronger, wiser, and more capable of forming and maintaining healthy and fulfilling relationships.

Throughout this book, we have explored various aspects of love and its connection to wisdom, drawing insights from the ancient Greek philosopher Plato. We have discussed the nature of love and how it shapes our lives, the different types of love, and the role of wisdom in sustaining healthy relationships.

We have seen how self-reflection and personal growth are crucial in the quest for wisdom in love, and how seeking knowledge and guidance from others can help us navigate the complexities of relationships. We have also examined the

---

[38] King, Stephen. 1977. The shining. N.p.: Knopf Doubleday Publishing Group.

importance of balance and the role of friendship in companionship.

Above all, we have emphasized the importance of wisdom in love. Wisdom enables us to make wise choices, understand the complexities of relationships, and navigate challenges with maturity and insight. It involves discerning qualities that are important for a healthy and sustainable relationship, such as mutual respect, trust, communication, and shared values.

In the pursuit of wisdom in love, we must remain committed to self-reflection, personal growth, and continuous learning. We must also strive to maintain a balance between the physical and spiritual aspects of love, recognizing the interconnectedness of these two realms.

As we navigate the complexities of love and relationships, we must draw from our own experiences, the experiences of others, and the wisdom of the ages. We must remain open-minded and compassionate, recognizing that each person's journey is unique and that there are no easy answers or quick fixes when it comes to matters of the heart.

Ultimately, the pursuit of wisdom in love is a lifelong journey, one that requires courage, patience, and perseverance. As we continue on this journey, may we be guided by the wisdom of the ages and the depths of our own hearts, and may we find meaning, purpose, and fulfillment in the pursuit of love.

Plato, the ancient Greek philosopher, has left an indelible mark on the realm of love and relationships. His insights into the nature of love, the role of wisdom, and the pursuit of meaning continue to resonate in modernity. Plato's philosophy of love, particularly his concept of Platonic love, has transcended time and continues to inspire and provoke thought in contemporary society.

In today's fast-paced and complex world, the wisdom of Plato's philosophy on love offers a timeless guide for navigating the intricacies of modern relationships. His emphasis on the importance of self-reflection, personal growth, and continuous learning serves as a reminder that wisdom in love is not a destination but a lifelong journey. Plato's recognition of the interconnectedness of the physical and spiritual aspects of love also serves as a reminder to seek a balance between these realms, valuing both the physical intimacy and the deeper emotional connection that love can offer.

Platonic love, in particular, has found resonance in modernity as a concept that goes beyond romantic or sexual love. It represents a pure and unconditional form of love that transcends physical desires and serves as an ideal to strive for in our relationships with others. In a world that is often characterized by superficial connections and fleeting romances, Plato's concept of Platonic love reminds us of the importance of cultivating deep and meaningful connections with others, based on mutual respect, understanding, and shared values.

In an era where relationships can be complex and challenging, Plato's insights on self-reflection, personal growth, seeking knowledge from others, the art of courtship, the importance of friendship, and the connection between love and beauty provide us with valuable lessons to navigate the complexities of modern relationships with wisdom and insight.

As we strive to find meaning and fulfillment in our relationships, may we draw inspiration from Plato's philosophy of love, and may his teachings continue to guide us in our pursuit of wisdom and love in the ever-evolving landscape of modernity.

END

****

www.ingramcontent.com/pod-product-compliance
Lightning Source LLC
Chambersburg PA
CBHW031424150726
47989CB00002B/793